SAFE

SAFE

How Priscilla and Ainie Grainger survived.
A story of domestic abuse, courage and escape.

SHANE DORAN

Published by:
Plan To Exit Safe Limited

ISBN 978-1-3999-3826-6

0Line Drawing of Priscilla and Ainie
by:
Jay O'Ceannobhain, Artist

Printed in Ireland
Naas Printing Ltd., Naas, Co. Kildare
Tel: (045) 872092
Email: naasprinting@gmail.com

2022

For Pat and Ann

This book is also dedicated to the women, men and child victims and survivors of domestic violence

Part of the proceeds of the sale of this book will be donated to various charities and support groups

CONTENTS

PRELUDE

'STOP THE fucking tears! Stop the fucking crying – you never stop fucking crying! What are you fucking crying for?'

Priscilla was lying face down on the bed in a state of shock, too numbed to move as the shouting got louder.

She tried to lift herself up, then he hit her again on the back.

The room was spinning. Priscilla thought she could see blue stars. She buried her head in the pillow, praying for it to end.

He got on the bed and kicked her in the back of her leg.

'Move fucking over – you're fucking useless.

'Go to sleep – you're fucking drunk!'

Priscilla closed her eyes, trying to shut out the pain and terror that enveloped her body and mind, like a virus spreading like wildfire inside her.

'How did it come to this?' she thought as she curled herself into a protective ball.

Part 1

ORIGINS

1

June 12, 1988
Drumcondra, Dublin

PAT GRAINGER sighed as his deep-set blue eyes surveyed the dirt and dust strewn across the floor of the building site that was now his home.

It would also somehow be the new family business in just two weeks. There was so much to be done, and so little time or money to do it.

It was almost too much to take in. Pat was exhausted, but as usual he didn't want to show it in front of Ann or Priscilla.

'I think we'll go for a jar.'

It was one of his favourite phrases, but this time there was no argument from his wife and daughter.

The Graingers had spent all day lugging what remained of their possessions into their new home, an old Georgian red brick on Drumcondra Road.

Their furniture was still in storage, but everything else was piled into the shell of a house that would become their home, their livelihood, their sanctuary.

Priscilla grimly examined the scene and turned to her mam: 'How in God's name are we going to turn this into a guesthouse in two weeks?'

Ann was tired but unfazed. Although tiny in stature, she had granite resolve; a no-nonsense Leitrim woman who had faced down some of Dublin's hardest criminals at the helm of several bars in the north inner city. She always knew what needed to be done and this time was no different.

'We've no bloody choice,' she said irritably. 'We've got to get it turned around – and we will.'

But there would be time for that in the morning. Right now, a drink sounded like a good idea.

The Graingers stepped out into the late summer evening and their spirits instantly lifted.

It was a beautiful and rare blue-sky evening and the bustle of the busy Dublin suburb felt exciting after the long years in the country.

Double decker buses and traffic whizzed by as they crossed the road and walked the short distance down the street to the pub.

Pat, in particular, had a spring in his step. He was a true blue, a Dubliner to the core and if felt good to be back in the city, despite the circumstances.

He'd been a barman and publican all his working life. It was all he knew, and he wasn't sure how he'd cope outside of the bar bubble. But now the guesthouse, which they named Leitrim House, was everything they owned, their only hope of getting back on their feet.

Priscilla felt a tremor of excitement as they walked into the bar. She was nervous but she felt secure. She always did with mam and dad, and this felt like a new beginning.

After three months huddled together in a cramped bedsit on the western outskirts of the city they were back close to their roots and with a place to call their own again.

They had a home and the makings of a business. She knew that's all it would take for mam and dad to start making money again.

Things would be ok, she told herself.

The pub was packed but the Graingers and friends who'd gathered to welcome them home managed to find a table in a corner of the bar.

Pat didn't sit down. He rarely did. Years working in inner-city pubs gave him a heightened sense of awareness, sometimes bordering on paranoia, but he had the mental and physical scars to remind him never to leave anything to chance. He refused to sit on a low stool or facing the wall. Pat always chose a high stool, directly facing the door. In control of the room.

The drinks flowed. Pat ordered a pint of Heineken and a Bushmills and ice for Ann. Priscilla cradled a bottle of Carlsberg as the joking and slagging kicked off.

Pat was getting the brunt of it, as usual, but he was well used to it.

'You've some hope of getting that job finished in time' … 'you should've gotten a contractor Pat!'

He laughed along but he knew he'd no choice in the matter. He had to get the place ready using direct labour. There was no money for a contractor, but he was happy to play the role of pretend skinflint.

The owner of the bar knew Pat well from the trade. He joined the company and one round followed another.

Priscilla was tired. She was enjoying the craic, but it had been a long day and she wanted to go home and crawl into her new makeshift bed. Pat called another round and convinced her to hang on for one more and they'd all go home together.

A barman arrived with the drinks. He looked directly at Priscilla but didn't say anything. She thought by the way he looked at her that they knew each other from somewhere.

He was nice looking fella, she thought. Dressed impeccably in his barman's uniform; crisp white shirt, black trousers, dicky bow.

There was something about him, the confident way he carried himself. The way he looked at her, almost familiar. A little unnerving, but Priscilla put it out of her mind. She was feeling a bit vulnerable and a little lost after upping sticks and unpacking her life again. She probably just fancied him a little.

Priscilla woke the next morning to the sound of builders downstairs clanging and banging her new home into some sort of shape. She felt a bit discombobulated but cheered up as she went downstairs and saw some familiar faces, lads who would have worked with her dad at various times down through the years.

Her father, as usual, was first up. Pat was an early riser, perennially in good form and cracking jokes no matter how early it was.

His wife was more of a night owl. Ann struggled down the stairs last, smiling to herself as she made a show of waving away her husband's annoying morning enthusiasm.

Anyway, there was work to be done.

Ann picked up the paper and began scanning the classifieds for bargains.

The Graingers had few possessions and little money left to buy what was needed to help transform the building into a fully functioning guesthouse.

She looked out for everything; little bits of second-hand furniture, things for the bathroom, used curtains. Ann was a talented seamstress. She couldn't afford to buy new curtains, but she could cut up old pieces of material, resize them to fit and make them good as new.

Pat played conductor of the DIY orchestra banging and clamouring its aggressive score through the house, but Ann silently took charge of the show.

Pat preferred to 'delegate' and liked to take the lads down to the pub for a pint after work.

Priscilla occasionally joined him. Her dad always cheered her up, no matter how down or lonely she was feeling.

But Pat was putting on a brave face. Behind the cheery optimism and the jokes, he was finding it difficult adjusting to life on the other side of the bar counter. It was all he knew, and he felt the loss badly.

He wouldn't speak about it, but Pat never got over losing the pubs. It was in his blood and he struggled to come to terms with his new station.

Then there was the money. Priscilla had to work extra jobs while also helping out at the B&B at weekends.

Ann missed the house. Their lost home, The Ward - called after the townland in Newtown Cross near the Dublin-Meath border on which it stood - was supposed to be the pinnacle of all their hard work, the prize for all the years they spent running pubs in some of Dublin's toughest inner-city neighbourhoods.

Pat and Ann purchased the site in 1979, four years after they returned to Dublin following a three-year stint in Limerick where they had bought their first pub.

They enjoyed their time in Limerick, but Pat was

restless. He wanted to get back to Dublin and fulfil his dream of following in his father's footsteps and see his own name above a premises in his home town.

He didn't have to wait too long. In 1975 he bought the iconic Five Lamps bar on the North Strand Road. Within three years he'd added Pat Grainger's pub in Ballybough and The Granby on Parnell Square to his burgeoning bar empire.

The Graingers enjoyed a lot of success and happy times in the early years.

Business was booming, but it was not all plain sailing. The life of an inner-city publican was not for the faint hearted.

Almost everyone who met Pat fell for his warm and easy-going nature, but he was no pushover. In the early days he was determined not to let local criminals who operated the protection rackets in the area call the shots.

Pat refused to hand over his money, but he ended up paying a heavy price. His car was burnt out on four separate occasions because he wouldn't play ball with the bullies.

The scourge of drugs and the crime wave that would come with it was yet to envelop the inner-city, but Pat and Ann had already begun to plan for the future.

After buying the site at The Ward the Graingers set about building their dream retirement home.

The house was impressive. Pat and Ann copied the design of Mount Vernon, the Vermont home of the first US President George Washington. Six imposing white pillars loomed over the entrance of the 5,000 sq/ft property. Inside, there was a wide, colonial-style staircase with red carpet, a lounge to the left, a large kitchen and utility room area and a study Pat used as an office. Upstairs there were four large bedrooms all boasting sweeping views of the Dublin-Meath hinterland.

The house was a veritable palace for Priscilla, who had spent most of her nine years living in cramped rooms above the family pubs.

It also became an idyllic escape from the inner-city which had become engulfed by a drug-fuelled crime wave that would devastate entire communities.

As the years went on The Ward became a refuge for Pat and the 6ft gentle giant loved nothing more than sitting on his ride-on mower basking in the country quiet on summer evenings.

By the early 1980s things had gotten much worse in the inner-city, and for the Graingers.

The break-ins, burglaries and constant threat of violence took a heavy toll on Pat. On more than one occasion he experienced the terror of having a gun pressed to his head as balaclava-clad raiders helped themselves to the takings.

Things got so bad Pat and Ann found it impossible to insure their premises and every robbery hit them hard in the pocket. They also took a heavy toll on Pat's mental health. She was only a child, but Priscilla clearly remembers the change coming over her father.

———

Dad suffered palpitations, he stopped working nights and became more withdrawn.

He would dread having to leave the house to go back into the city. 'Back into the concrete feckin' jungle – back into the head cases,' he'd say.

Mam would have given it all up too, but she knew they couldn't afford to yet. She'd say to him, 'these head cases are paying for all this so we've got to keep going.'

We'd had some great years; we were living in luxury compared to what we were used to, but the times were changing.

Security became a huge issue; dad's biggest fear was that I would be kidnapped or raped – the threats were that bad.

I remember one morning dad saying to mam: 'I can't get up, I'm not able for it anymore.'

'Well,' she says, 'I'm not going in on my own so you may get up – we're in this together.'

But it was clear dad didn't have the stomach for it anymore. His nerves were shot. Mam stepped into the breach. Dad took a step back and she took over the running of the pubs.

It was pretty daunting for a woman back then, but mam is a formidable woman.

She rolled up her sleeves and this slight five-foot woman from the bogs of Leitrim didn't take any shite! And they respected her for it, even the gougers [running protection rackets].

She wouldn't hand over cash to them, but she'd pay them in pints when she had to. It worked too; the hard men respected her and got on well with her and they wouldn't let anyone else mess with her, or with us.

———

Eventually, though, it became too much - even for Ann - as inner-city neighbourhoods were transformed into battle grounds and communities were sucked into increasingly violent turf wars that played out on their streets.

In 1983 the pub in Ballybough was set on fire again. Pat and Ann had no insurance, and their financial situation had become precarious. They were living in relative luxury in The Ward, but their income was drying up and things looked likely to get worse before they got any better.

Not long afterwards they decided they had enough and began to withdraw from the city to move closer to their dream retirement home.

In 1985 they sold the pubs and retreated lock, stock and barrel out of Dublin, to Navan.

Kilcarn House was a roadhouse bar just outside the county Meath town that was becoming popular with a rising tide of Dublin dwellers looking to move out of the city.

Pat and Ann had seen the premises for sale and thought it had great potential. It was just up the road from The Ward and seemed a million miles from the inner-city and the violence that had pushed the Dublin publican out of his natural habitat.

Pat threw himself into the new venture. He ploughed their savings and whatever they had left from the sale of the pubs into his new bar.

Pat rediscovered his mojo. Ann and Priscilla, who was now 18, were infected by his new-found enthusiasm and set about making their new adventure a success.

Kilcarn House was to be Pat and Ann's legacy, something they could leave behind for Priscilla to take over.

But Navan was a disaster. Almost everything that could go wrong did, right from the start.

Pat's gregarious personality meant he was well-liked by almost everyone who met him, and Navan was no different. But to locals the Graingers were always regarded as outsiders. Dubs. Blow-ins.

They had problems with some local guards, who would often come around expecting free drink or food 'as if they owned the place.'

It drove Ann mad. She preferred dealing with some of the inner city hardmen; at least they showed her a bit of respect.

The location, on the outskirts of the town on the side of a main road, was also poor and Pat and Ann struggled to pull the punters in.

There were a few hairy incidents. The Graingers thought they had left crime behind them in the inner-city but by now pubs and cash businesses on the outskirts of the capital found themselves being targeted.

One night as they slept the pub was broken into and the takings stolen. On another occasion their car was set alight.

Pat and Ann were crestfallen. They thought they had left all this behind; now it felt as if the trouble had followed them out of Dublin.

But Pat was determined to make a success of it. He dug in and continued to pump what little was left of their savings into the pub.

Within three years the dream had turned into a nightmare. The Graingers were in trouble. Kilcarn House had become a money pit, draining their dwindling resources and threatening to wipe out their life's work.

Payments were missed. Letters from the bank begun to pile up, each one more menacing than the last.

The situation had become hopeless. The Graingers were about to lose their pub – and their beautiful home.

Pat was devastated. His gamble had failed badly, and he felt he had left his wife and daughter down.

Ann and Priscilla didn't feel that way, despite their own disappointment. They loved Pat more than anything and still believed they could somehow climb out of the hole they found themselves in.

But their financial situation only got worse and as time went on, with the banks circling, Ann knew they had no choice but to part with their beloved home.

After selling The Ward the Graingers moved in with their close friend and neighbours, the McLaughlins, for a few weeks and most of their remaining possessions were put into storage.

Shortly afterwards they gravitated back to Dublin, this time to a tiny granny flat in Roselawn on the western outskirts of the city, which they could barely afford.

It was a far cry from the luxury and space they enjoyed in the country, but despite their new circumstances they didn't despair.

Priscilla was 21, no longer heiress to a bar business and beautiful country pile. But she was a hard worker and believed it was only a matter of time before the family would turn things around.

With no money and only their years of experience in the pub trade to fall back on, Pat and Ann made plans to emigrate to the UK. Ann made contact with several British breweries and the Graingers received a tentative offer to become licensees of a public house in Watford, on the outskirts of north London.

The Graingers didn't want to leave the country, but it seemed they had no option and so they began preparing for a new and very different life in England.

Then, out of the blue, they were thrown a lifeline. Ann had been involved in a car accident some months beforehand, and just as they were about to make their reluctant move across the water a cheque arrived for £30,000. With the leftovers from the sale of The Ward, it was enough to make a new start.

After a few weeks Pat and Ann found a property back near the inner-city from where they came, albeit it in leafy Drumcondra, that they could just about afford.

No 55 Upper Drumcondra Road was a large red-brick property on the main airport road out of the city. The Georgian period house was in bad repair, but in the perfect location to build a B&B business.

It wasn't the dream ending the Graingers envisaged three years earlier when they thought they had left the inner-city for good.

But they had been given another chance and this time they were determined to make it work.

2

DESPTE THE initial excitement, the first few months were difficult.

Somehow Pat, Ann, Priscilla and their little army of builders manged to transform the building site into a fully functioning guesthouse within two weeks. They didn't have a choice; they had a wedding party booked and Ann was adamant they would not let their first guests down.

It was hard work, but they threw themselves into their new project. They didn't have time to dwell on the previous few months and it was like a form of therapy.

The little family was happy working together. Money was tight, but they managed.

Pat, Ann and Priscilla crammed themselves and most of their remaining possessions into a single bedroom. Priscilla slept on a mattress on the floor beside the bed.

They didn't have a proper kitchen in the early days, so meals would be grabbed on the run or across the road in the pub when there was enough money.

Just weeks after facing the prospect of bankruptcy, the Graingers were back in business. It was slow to begin with, but bit by bit the bookings started coming in.

Pat and Ann settled into a new routine. But they were all, in their own way, struggling to adapt to their new lives. Pat, for all his optimism, felt the most pain. All his working life had been spent behind a bar counter, his ambition and dreams were irrevocably intertwined with the pub trade. He knew his family was fighting for survival and he felt responsible for their new circumstances.

Aside from Ann and Priscilla, the pubs were his life. He desperately wanted to be able to provide for his family and it hurt to see his daughter having to take on so much work at such a young age.

For Ann and Priscilla, the loss of The Ward was the hardest to come to terms with.

One night Ann came home to find her husband and daughter down in the dumps and, for once, she broke.

The tension had been building for weeks and needed a release. They all cried, the first tears any of them had shed for a long time. They talked together about their loss, the pain of the past few months, and what lay ahead.

It didn't take Ann long to regain her composure. She dried her eyes and turned to Pat and Priscilla: 'We lost our beautiful home and I miss it. I miss the bedrooms, the reception rooms, the kitchen, the beautiful gardens. But this is how it is and we have to struggle on. We have each other and we've got to accept it.

'We've got a mortgage to pay to keep this roof over our heads. We've all had a bad day, but so what?

'Tomorrow will be better if we make it.'

Priscilla began to come out of her own and her parents' protective shell. She missed her friends back in the country but didn't have the time or money to visit them. She dusted herself down and resolved to make a go of her new life.

Priscilla inherited her parents' entrepreneurial spirit and set up her own business providing secretarial services.

She rented a small office space above a shop in Drumcondra, just a few doors up from the pub, where Priscilla would sometimes go for lunch or, if it was a good week, a few drinks after work on Friday.

The handsome barman she'd briefly encountered that first night in Drumcondra would be there most days. Sometimes they'd chat for a while, making small talk until it became uncomfortable.

Priscilla grew in confidence. She was naturally outgoing like her dad and her warm, trusting personality meant she made friends easily.

Then, mostly due to her dad's encouragement, she decided to get involved in local politics.

Pat was a Fianna Fáil man, even though some in his family leaned more towards Fine Gael.

When the Graingers moved to Drumcondra, Fianna Fáil's local O'Donovan Rossa Cumann was the power base for a politician who would go on to dominate politics in Ireland for over a decade.

On July 12, 1989, newly elected Taoiseach Charlie Haughey formed a new government with the Progressive Democrats. His Cabinet contained two Drumcondra residents who lived just yards either side of the Graingers' new home.

Ray Burke, whose home on Griffith Downs was just around the corner from Number 55, was appointed Minister for Communications. Burke's political career would end in acrimony, his name eventually becoming synonymous with planning tribunals.

Haughey's other local ministerial appointment lived on the opposite end of the suburban village in a modest house in Beresford Avenue. He would also go on to create many headlines of his own but would have a far more significant role to play in Irish life. The new Minister for Labour, Bertie Ahern, was a rising star in the party, but few would have tipped the northside Dubliner, often pilloried in the press as 'anorak man', to go on to lead three-successive governments.

Few outside of Drumcondra, that is. Many of those in Bertie's close circle of friends and political allies in Drumcondra at the time believed he was destined for great things.

Priscilla certainly did. As she became immersed in local politics, she forged strong friendships and relationships with Bertie's team, some of whom would later become known as the 'Drumcondra mafia' in media and political circles when Ahern became embroiled in the 'dig out' revelations into his private finances.

There was Tony Kett, Bertie's close friend and confidante who would go on to take his seat on Dublin Corporation and become a senator; Paul Kiely, the former chief executive of the Central Remedial Clinic; Paddy 'The Plasterer' Reilly; Tim Collins, another childhood friend; Fianna Fáil fundraiser Des Richardson; Jim Nugent, a former director of the Central Bank of Ireland and chairman of CERT, the State tourism training agency.

Priscilla knew them all and liked most of them. She was impressed with their dedication, resourcefulness and ruthless loyalty to 'The Chief'.

And she adored Bertie. When she first met the future Taoiseach, his office was a single small room above Fagan's pub in Drunmcondra, directly across the road from St Luke's, the imposing red brick doctor's surgery that would later become Ahern's constituency headquarters.

It was shortly before the 1989 general election and Bertie's tiny office was a hive of activity. A queue of constituents, volunteers and party activists stretched from the cramped room to the street below.

Pat Grainger had known Bertie from his time as Lord Mayor of Dublin. The two men shared a deep respect, bordering on reverence, for the elderly. Pat organised Christmas parties for pensioners in the inner city and Bertie was always glad to help out whenever needed, as were former Independent TD Tony Gregory and local councillor Christy Burke.

Bertie liked and respected Pat and when Priscilla told him who she was he immediately invited her to join his team of volunteers.

Within days Priscilla was out pounding the pavements with Bertie's team on the canvass; knocking on doors, talking to constituents, discussing their concerns, finding ways to help.

It opened up a whole new world to Priscilla. She was happy and felt she was making a difference.

———

I loved canvassing with Bertie. The amount of work he did for the people in the constituency was incredible. He knew every name and every door, who they were, how they voted, what their issues were.

Bertie's team had a great system in place to make sure every house in the constituency was covered. He had a ward boss who would be in charge of a particular area that could have up to 20,000 constituents, and they would be in charge of a little team of volunteers. I was on one of those teams, one of the spokes [of the wheel]. We'd knock on the doors and say, 'good afternoon'. Bertie never knocked on any door after nine o'clock at night – as soon as the news came on you had to close the gate and even if that gate was open when you arrived up you always closed it on the way out.

There would be great banter on the streets. You might run into some of the opposition [rival candidates] – and some of these would have been other Fianna Fáilers who were running against Bertie for the same seat

After nine o'clock we'd go back to the office and go through the constituency sheets, we used to call them query sheets. We'd hand them over to the secretaries and Bertie would go through the sheets and see what needed to be done for them. Bertie had a great, great respect for the vulnerable in his constituency, particularly the elderly. You might have somebody who was living in really primitive conditions and Bertie would turn around to one of the councillors and say: 'I'm not happy with Mrs Murphy's situation – she needs to be looked after.'

In those days there was no emails, mobile phones, Facebook ... nothing like that. It was all one-to-one, the personal touch, shaking hands. How are you? What can we do for you? That's what it was all about.

I remember one time I knocked on a door and this auld fella said to me: 'I lost me false teeth – is there anything Bertie can do for me?'

And he did, Bertie somehow got that man a new set of teeth – and his vote.

Another night I knocked on a door and I asked this lady to give Bertie her number one [vote]. She turned to me and says: 'I'm giving no one my number f**king one – I'm onto Dublin f**king Corporation for the last two years about my toilet seat, I've no toilet seat.'

I went back to the office and explained the problem. Bertie told one of the lads in the office to 'go down to the hardware shop and pick up a toilet seat and go down to that woman and put it on for her if she needs it.' In those days it was sometimes difficult to get hold of the right people in Dublin Corporation over small constituency problems so Bertie would often just get one of his team to sort it out there and then, and he'd pay for it himself. That was what made Bertie special.

Bertie Ahern was also impressed with the young volunteer's work ethic and her hands-on approach when it came to solving constituency problems.

Priscilla's naturally competitive spirit was a good fit for the cumann, which actively encouraged rivalry between its wards that focused on different parts of the constituency.

Bertie's team regarded themselves as social activists more than political ideologues. They preferred to focus on practical constituency issues that could make a difference to people on the ground – and win their vote.

And, Bertie recalls, Priscilla's personality was a perfect fit for the ethos of his political organisation.

Even though she was very young, Priscilla knew the game; she understood the issues and was very good at canvassing.

She liked to resolve problems and to get her teeth into things, bringing people together, getting things done rather than just talking about it.

She was all go, go, go in terms of her attitude.

We had a rule that if anyone came to us or asked us for something, our obligation was to check it out and do something about it, not to prejudge it or to say, 'that's rubbish.'

We followed everything up and Priscilla was very good at understanding the importance of that. Our view was that: 'If someone asks for something, get an answer.' If you couldn't solve it, at least get an answer.

We considered ourselves activists; it was all about action. We didn't see ourselves as a talking shop. Our meetings were under the lamppost at 7pm. People who were interested in being active, joined. People who were interested in talking, didn't ... probably because they thought we were all nuts.

And we made it fun. There was a great social element to it. We had barbecues, Christmas parties ... if there was any [excuse for a] party, we'd have a party!

There was also great competition between the different wards. Thankfully – now I can say it all these years later – we were never too worried about getting elected, because we knew we would get elected. But the craic was that; would Drumcondra South C [ward] beat Glasnevin A? There was fierce competition within the group and that led to great rivalry, but great fun as well.

As Bertie Ahern's political career soared, Priscilla's personal life blossomed. By now she had a wide circle of friends, and her confidence was growing.

After a few weeks on the canvass Priscilla began to find her feet. Literally. She struck up a close friendship with a young woman her own age and the pair would go dancing together, often several times a week, at their favourite clubs, Rumours and the Mont Clare.

One Sunday night at the Mont Clare Priscilla bumped into the barman from the local pub in Drumcondra, who was also with a friend.

Priscilla had gotten to know him a little from being in the bar, but it was usually just harmless banter.

Tonight was a bit different. Priscilla knew she liked him and, with a bit of Dutch courage, asked him if he'd like to come to her cousin's 21st party.

He didn't give a yes or a no: 'Hmmm, maybe if I'm not doing anything I will.'

Priscilla found his response odd, and a bit annoying, but she didn't know anything about him and let it pass.

Later, as Priscilla was finishing her drink, the barman turned to her and said: 'Ah sure, I'll do ye a favour and go with ye to the party.'

She thought it was probably just his sense of humour. Priscilla was happy, feeling more confident than ever and now she had a date to look forward to. He asked her to dance, and later for her number. They got a taxi home together and he told her he'd give her a call.

He rang the next day and they went out for a drink, which turned into a few. They met again the same week and then every Tuesday and Thursday when the barman wasn't working.

Priscilla was smitten.

He treated her like a queen and had impeccable manners. He would always organise a stool for her at the bar and offer to get the drinks. He was confident, charming and seemed to get on with everybody. He loved to joke and laugh and lavished Priscilla with attention. Pretty soon she was swept off her feet.

Shortly after they began dating Priscilla invited him to Leitrim House for tea to meet her parents.

Ann and Pat also fell for the charming barman with perfect manners, and this was the icing on the cake for Priscilla.

Pat already knew the barman and they'd occasionally chatted in the pub, swapping war stories about the trade.

More importantly, Pat and Ann saw Priscilla was happier than she'd been for a long time.

Business was also picking up. The Graingers felt as if they were on the road to recovery after almost losing everything.

3

PRISCILLA FELT troubled.

In the space of a few weeks, she'd set up her own business, become immersed in local politics and fallen in love for the first time.

She was convinced he felt the same.

He showered her with affection and attention, and it was intoxicating. They saw each other every day and it felt as if the phone was never off the hook when they were apart.

But now he was about to emigrate to Australia. He'd told Priscilla shortly after they met about his travel plans, but now things were beginning to get serious.

She told him she loved him, and he said he felt the same way. But now he was preparing to move to the other side of the world.

Priscilla was crushed. She didn't want him to go but he was adamant. His brother was in Australia and he was going to live and work out there for a year. It was all arranged.

Priscilla tried to put it out of her mind and make the most of the time they had together, but it was always there in the background. They went out on dates, to restaurants, to the cinema, the pub.

They never stayed in. Priscilla secretly wanted them to share a few relaxing nights in together, but he always insisted on going out.

They went away on weekends together. Down to Cork, to Priscilla's maternal home in Leitrim and, after just six weeks together, on a romantic getaway to London. Priscilla was having a great time, but the shadow of Australia loomed large in the background.

She also began to notice a different side to him, little things she would later dismiss as being unimportant or just down to her overthinking.

He loved the high life. The partying. The designer clothes. But he never seemed to have much money.

Priscilla wasn't exactly flush. She was working hard, and the family was just getting back on their collective feet, but she had a better handle on finances.

He always seemed happy to put everything on the credit card. Or to let Priscilla pay.

It was her first time, during that weekend away in London. It wasn't what she expected, but she tried to hide her disappointment and told herself she just wasn't ready. Next time would be different.

Priscilla detected a slight change in him afterwards.

He seemed a bit more territorial towards her, but she put this down to him being more confident.

She tried not to overthink it. She finally had a boyfriend, someone who loved her, and Priscilla lost herself in the fairy tale of the romance. She dreamed of a white dress wedding and the family they would have together.

Then he was gone.

He flew to Australia in March 1990. Priscilla was heartbroken but she believed in him and never thought this would be the end.

He said he'd be back in 12 months and they agreed – at his suggestion – not to see anyone else while they were apart.

Once he got to Australia, he initially called her several times every week, including every Saturday night when Priscilla would otherwise have been out with friends.

He wrote regularly too, and his letters gave Priscilla the impression he was deeply committed to her.

In one dispatch he told Priscilla his time away would give her a good opportunity 'to start saving' for the future. She took this to be a shared commitment and began squirreling away whatever she could.

Priscilla worked long hours and several different jobs; her secretarial business, in the guesthouse and wherever she could pick up a few extra hours. Within a few months she had a few grand saved.

But as the months dragged by the phone calls began to taper off. Priscilla became worried.

One weekend she called his brother directly when he failed to respond to her calls.

His brother assured her everything was ok. He was just busy with work.

But Priscilla wasn't entirely convinced.

When he did eventually call back more than 48 hours later, he tried to shrug off his absence and became angry when Priscilla tried to pursue it.

She was acting 'crazy', he told her, while he was working hard for the two of them. Priscilla blamed herself and put it down to her missing him so much.

Then in December, out of the blue, he announced he was coming home, three months earlier than planned.

He didn't say why but Priscilla didn't care. She was overjoyed and they would soon be back together.

They planned to meet in London and spend a few days together before flying back to Dublin.

Priscilla did all the running. She booked the hotel and the flights and, in her own mind, the fun nights ahead as they planned their rest of their life together.

Priscilla had kept her part of the bargain and saved up a nice little nest egg, but when she met him in London it was obvious he was penniless.

Her boyfriend had promised to come back with at least £10,000 saved for their new life together. But, he told her, it was difficult getting work in Australia and he ran out of money.

Priscilla was disappointed and a bit peeved, but she was so happy to see him and tried not to let it overshadow the reunion.

His financial situation didn't get any better when they got back to Dublin.

Ireland, despite the feelgood factor in the aftermath of Italia '90, was coming out of a deep recession and the barman struggled to find work.

His old job had been filled. Many pubs across the city were closing and it was hard to find a full-time gig, but he didn't seem all that bothered.

He managed to pick up a few shifts here and there, but nothing regular. The Graingers had recently set up their own catering company and Pat offered him work as a sales rep, but he hated it and only lasted a few days on the job.

Priscilla's savings, the money she'd put away for their new life, quickly evaporated as she found herself picking up the tab for their nights out.

She became worried. He seemed different since he came back from Australia, more downbeat. Priscilla felt some of the spark had gone out of him.

He could still turn on the charm at the drop of a hat, but he was prone to mood swings. And sometimes he could be short with Priscilla, seemingly for no reason.

She tried to placate him and put it down to work and money, or the lack of both.

Priscilla began to notice a few other things that concerned her. When they were in company with people he knew he never introduced her. It would leave her feeling deflated, but he would dismiss it. She was 'imagining things'.

He also didn't like Priscilla's friends, especially her Fianna Fáil comrades, and he wasn't shy about letting his feelings be known.

They were all 'arseholes' or 'know-it-alls', not to be trusted. He was the only one she could rely on.

Priscila was in love, but she got tired of the moods and of her boyfriend never having any money.

I was really disappointed. I had planned and saved so hard for our future and our life together and it felt like he came back a changed person.

I couldn't see any future, there was no drive in him, and he wasn't being proactive about anything. Everything was negative.

I had to do all the running. He couldn't even drive at this point and was going from job to job.

It was as if he came back from Australia a different person. I wanted to go out there to visit him, but he didn't want me to and he was very cagey with me about his life over there, he never liked talking about it.

I didn't feel loved, and I was worried about the future. We talked about getting a place of our own but it felt like we were a million miles away from getting a deposit for a house.

———

Finally, Priscilla decided she had enough.

In early December 1991 she called her boyfriend down to the house. She told him it wasn't working and that the relationship was over.

He got angry and stormed out.

Priscilla was heartbroken but resolved to get on with her life. She started going out with her friends again, back dancing at Rumours and the Mont Clare.

But he wouldn't let her go.

Shortly before Christmas he unexpectedly called to her house with a present. He asked her out for one quick drink, just to show there were 'no hard feelings'.

Priscilla's armour buckled. And by the end of the night they were back together.

In the weeks and months that followed he seemed a changed man. Or at least the man she originally fell for.

His mood was more upbeat. He learned to drive. He was working full time as head barman at another pub on the northside. He was talking about saving money for a deposit again. But this time things would be different, he insisted.

He also helped out with the guesthouse when Pat and Ann needed a hand.

Priscilla was delighted. The relationship was back on track and she began planning for their future again.

Around this time Priscilla got an unexpected windfall. A few months earlier she slipped on a wet floor at a fast-food restaurant in the city-centre, damaging the small of her back.

Then, just as they had begun saving for their first home, a cheque for £25,000 arrived in the post.

Pat convinced Priscilla to put the money into a high-interest savings account that charged high penalties for early withdrawal. Their deposit seemed secured.

But Priscilla and her boyfriend were enjoying the high-life again and, despite now having a full-time job, he still never seemed to have any money.

Priscilla suspected he might be gambling, but he always had an excuse. 'The father isn't well' ... 'my mother needed a loan'.

Priscilla was burning through the cash as well and their savings dried up as the money evaporated into a cloud of partying, weekends away and long nights out.

Eventually he persuaded Priscilla to withdraw her compensation money, despite the financial penalties.

He told her they could put the money into a joint current account to save for the house.

Priscilla agreed. Then they went on holiday to Portugal.

The money was running out fast.

Priscilla was having a great time but the dream of owning their own home seemed as distant as ever.

In December 1993, 12 months after they briefly separated, they met for a drink at the Skylon Hotel, just down the road from the guesthouse.

He told Priscilla he wanted to buy a house.

'With what?' she replied. 'We don't have nearly enough saved?'

He took a sip from his pint.

'We'll talk to your father about where we can afford to buy,' he said, before landing the bombshell: 'Why don't we get engaged for Christmas?'

Priscilla's heart stopped a beat.

Was he really asking her to marry him?

She looked at him and laughed as she was overcome by a wave of contrasting emotions.

Priscilla wanted nothing more than to marry him, to have their own home and family.

But this wasn't how she imagined a proposal. No going down on the bended knee, not even a ring.

'Go into town and pick out a ring for yourself,' he said, as if reading her thoughts.

———

I think I was in a state of shock.

I suppose I was a bit old fashioned in that I thought when people got married there was a bit of magic to it.

Yes, I was disappointed, but I was confused because this was what I had wanted all along and he knew this.

He knew I wanted to get married, to have a family and a house, but he didn't have any money – at the time he'd have struggled to get the bus fare to the airport.

I called a friend of mine, and we went down to Brereton's Jeweller's on O'Connell Street and picked out a ring.

That night we went out for a meal with his brother and his wife and then back to the Skylon for a few drinks.

I told my parents shortly afterwards, but they already had a fair idea. They were delighted, they really liked him.

I felt happy but I wasn't fully sure of myself. I was 25 at the time. It was probably wrong of me to look at it that way, but I did worry.

We had another night out to celebrate with mam and dad and a few friends.

His brothers and sisters came down, but he didn't want his parents to know. I didn't know why, it seemed as if he didn't want my parents to meet them.

4

IF PRISCILLA'S new fiancé was hoping his proposal would help towards the deposit, Pat Grainger didn't disappoint.

In fact, he didn't even have to broach the subject with his father-in-law to be.

The following Sunday he was invited to Leitrim House for tea.

Pat got straight to the point.

'Well,' he said, 'have you decided what you're doing to do about a house?'

Priscilla was relieved, but she felt bad her dad had to come to the rescue. She knew her fiancé had little more than a grand saved. Without help from her parents they didn't have a hope of getting a deposit together.

But Pat didn't mind. He was adamant his daughter would not be getting married unless she had the security of her own home.

'You'll never get ahead of the system if you don't,' he told them.

Pat estimated their combined wages, together with the deposit, meant they could just about afford a mortgage of £50,000.

Priscilla was happy and Pat was relieved, after the guilt he felt over the loss of their old home and business, that he was able to help his daughter when she needed it most.

Then, as the couple were busy planning for their new home and wedding, disaster struck.

In February 1993 Pat was diagnosed with Wegener's disease, now more commonly known as Granulomatosis with polyangiitis (GPA), a rare and life-threatening blood disorder.

Priscilla and Ann were devastated but they rallied around Pat, who underwent a battery of tests as his health deteriorated.

Priscilla took over much of the running of the guesthouse and the catering business, trying to save and prepare for her wedding while keeping a positive side out for her dad.

Her fiancé also stepped up to the plate, much to her relief.

———

He was a great help to us with the business, and a great help to mam too.

He regularly went to see dad when he was in hospital and would stay talking to him for long periods.

He showed a great side of the type of man he could be. He had a very difficult time with his parents and he kind of adopted mine.

———

Despite his declining health, Pat continued to help his daughter and her fiancé to find a home. In September, while he was in hospital, Pat told Priscilla he found the perfect place.

The house was in a newish development of mostly three-bed semis just off the Navan Road near the Phoenix Park. The house, and the £52,000 price tag, was perfect for Priscilla and her fiancé, and not too far from her parents' guesthouse in Drumcondra.

Pat gave the couple £5,000 and used his banking contacts to help them secure the mortgage.

Priscilla had saved £2,500 but she knew they would need more money to furnish the house. Then there was the wedding and honeymoon.

She got the keys to her new home in March 1994, but they put off moving in until after they were married so they could use the rental income as savings.

It was a hectic few months as Priscilla juggled the demands of the business, her father's declining health, renovating her new home and the small matter of the wedding.

She was running the catering business on her own, while Ann struggled to keep the guesthouse going without her husband and partner.

In the end, it became too much, and Pat and Ann decided to sell Leitrim House, the home and business that had become their refuge and saviour after almost losing everything.

They sold the guesthouse and bought a house on the Navan Road, less than a kilometre up the road from Priscilla's new home.

They moved into the house, which they called Leitrim Lodge, in July 1995, just a month before the wedding.

Despite his ill-health, Pat threw himself into his new project and rallied all the troops he needed to get the house into shape ahead of his daughter's big day. Within three weeks his new home was completely refurbished and the gardens newly landscaped.

Priscilla was relieved her parents would be so close by, particularly given Pat's health. It made things easier for them and she wanted to spend as much time as she could with her dad, just in case.

The move and approaching wedding lifted everyone's spirits, especially Pat's.

He arranged a stag do for his son-in-law to be, a day of racing at The Curragh with his brothers and some friends from the bar trade.

Afterwards, the stag party ended up back at the Skylon Hotel, where they were joined by Priscilla and Ann.

It was a great night, Priscilla remembers, full of fun and laughter, but bittersweet too. Everything was changing, they were on the move again.

Priscilla looked across the room as Pat led the party in another singsong.

She couldn't imagine life without him.

Priscilla was excited about the wedding, but she was left to do all the planning.

Her fiancé appeared upbeat too, but beyond getting fitted up for his suit he was happy to leave everything to Priscilla.

She became concerned about his family. Priscilla had met his parents a few times but found it hard to warm to them. His mother seemed nice but a bit distant, almost cowed. She took an instant dislike to his father, a gruff, unsmiling man who didn't appear to have a good word for anyone.

He often, her fiancé told her, took the belt to him and his siblings when they were younger when the mood took him. Priscilla thought of her fiancé's own mood swings and occasional lapses into darkness and silently made her calculation.

Outwardly religious, his father had ruled the family home with an iron first. His word was law, and his children paid a painful price if they disobeyed.

Priscilla thought it was strange they didn't hear anything from his parents in the countdown to the wedding. No invite to come over to the house for dinner or a drink. No offer to help with any of the events planned for the big day.

Ann decided to break the unspoken silence and invited her soon-to-be son-in-law's family over to Leitrim Lodge for a get together three days before the wedding.

It was one of those rare, perfect Irish summer days and the two families sat outside in the back garden enjoying the chat and the sunshine.

Except for his father, who complained constantly, even more so after an apple from a tree above fell on his head.

Priscilla and Ann bit their lips and did their best to keep from laughing.

The apple, Priscilla noted, hadn't even fallen that far from the tree.

The day before the wedding Priscilla was a bag of nerves and excitement.

Pat arranged a big family gathering at Leitrim Lodge and the house was overflowing with food, drink, friends, relatives and laughter.

Priscilla was anxious, but she talked herself around. It's just nerves, she told herself, I'll be grand once I get down that bloody aisle.

She was in town with her fiancé because he wanted to get a last-minute haircut.

Priscilla drove him into the city centre and parked the car on Townsend Street while he said he was popping into a nearby barbers across the road from the bookies.

The minutes passed, then an hour. Priscilla became worried, then angry that he'd left her sitting on her own with so much to do just hours before the wedding.

Eventually, after an hour and a half, he returned. His hair appeared unchanged.

Priscilla was exasperated.

'Where the hell were ye?'

Her fiancé snapped, turning on her. And for the first time since she'd known him, he raised his voice in a threatening manner.

'What do ye mean where was I? You know where I was,' he shouted at her.

Priscilla struggled to hold back the tears.

How could he speak to me like this ... the day before our wedding?

She felt herself shaking as she drove them back to the Navan Road while he simmered beside her making small talk.

Later, once everyone had left, Pat said he needed to go to bed.

He had his bloods done earlier and was worn out from the excitement.

He turned to Priscilla, smiling.

'It's your big day tomorrow love; I'll leave you with your mam.'

Priscilla's stomach lurched. Every bone in her body was telling her something was wrong, but she didn't want to worry her dad.

'Yeah, isn't it great,' she said as he waved goodnight and struggled up the stairs.

———

Dad was very sick, and I knew, there and then, that he wasn't going to make it.

It was my wedding the next day but all I could think about was, 'how long will I have him?'

It was just me and mam then, together downstairs, everyone had gone. Suddenly I burst into tears, I couldn't hold it back anymore.

I said to mam: 'I don't know if I can go through with this.'

She looked me straight in the eye and said 'why?'

'I don't know, there's something telling me not to.'

Mam told me: 'If you don't want to get married there's nothing stopping you from calling it all off right now.

'You can make the call this minute – it's not too late. Your dad can make the phone call for you right now, no one will be left short. But you have to tell him [fiancé].'

I hadn't touched a drink all night, but my mind was all over the place. I couldn't think clearly.

'Maybe it's just the nerves, maybe I'm just nervous.'

'I can't tell you,' mam said to me. 'You're the only person who can answer that.'

I asked her what she thought of him [fiancé].

She told me: 'You're not going to ask me that the night before your wedding. I think he's a lovely guy, but you've got to make that decision.'

It felt as if the room was spinning. I felt sick. I got up to go to the toilet.

I could feel something in the pit of my stomach, but I tried to ignore it. Maybe I'm being a drama queen, making a mountain out of nothing.

I wanted everything to be ok. I wanted to marry him, even if I knew it wasn't going to be the fairy-tale. Sure what marriage is?

I dried my eyes and came out of the toilet.

I looked at mam.

'No, it's just nerves,' I said.

'Definitely. I'll be fine.'

Part 2

HONEYMOON

5

'STOP THE the fucking tears! Stop the fucking crying – you never stop fucking crying! What are you fucking crying for?'

Priscilla was lying face down on the bed in a state of shock, too numbed to move as the shouting got louder.

She tried to lift herself up, then he hit her again on the back.

The room was spinning. Priscilla thought she could see blue stars. She buried her head in the pillow, praying for it to end.

He got on the bed and kicked her in the back of her leg.

'Move fucking over – you're fucking useless.

'Go to sleep – you're fucking drunk!'

Priscilla closed her eyes, trying to shut out the pain and terror that enveloped her body and mind, like a virus spreading like wildfire inside her.

She lay there frozen. She didn't utter a sound or move a muscle until she heard the snores.

Silently, she crept out of the bed and tippy-toed her way out of the room and down two flights of stairs to the hotel lobby.

It was after 3am in Florida, the third night of their honeymoon, but mam and dad would still be up at home. She needed to hear their voices.

Pat and Ann came on the phone, surprised at the lateness of the call.

'Are you ok love?'

'I'm grand, I just wanted to let you know we got here and that I'm safe.'

Her voice faltered. She knew she couldn't keep up the pretence for long.

'I'm wrecked ... just wanted to check in with yis. I'll give ye a call in a day or two.'

Priscilla shuddered as she reluctantly hung up the phone.

She would never feel safe again.

6

IT WAS a perfect day for a wedding.

The day arrived at the tail end of Ireland's hottest summer on record. Temperatures soared in the weeks leading up to the big day as the country basked in rare Mediterranean sunshine.

By Friday the mercury had dipped a little, leaving the slightest of breezes as a sultry blue-sky hung over Dublin, illuminating a city more used to the greys and cloud-covered dreariness of its oceanic climate.

Priscilla woke early. She didn't get much sleep, but she felt alive as the glow of sunlight filled the room. She hoped it was a sign.

Her nerves turned to excitement as the room suddenly erupted in a fog of wedding chaos.

Bodies, bridesmaids at first, then the rest, descended on Priscilla. Loud, excitable voices had bewildered pets hiding for cover.

Priscilla felt as if she was in a dream as she was lifted out of the bed, then on to the hairdressers and beauticians.

By the time she got home everyone was dressed.

The house was heaving with family and friends. There was food and drink everywhere and the sound of laughter filled the air.

Priscilla loved the chaos. She wasn't one for ceremony and didn't give a damn who saw her in the dress beforehand.

She looked at her parents.

Ann was wearing a beautiful navy and lemon suit Pat bought her as a special treat during a trip to Paris that March. It caught her eye as she was browsing in a boutique on the Champs Elysees. It was expensive, far more than Ann would have paid, but Pat insisted.

'We've only one daughter, we'll only have one day like this so I'm buying it for you.'

Pat didn't pay as much attention to his own attire.

As the wedding party was milling around the kitchen in mutual admiration, Priscilla noticed her dad's suit trousers were a full eight inches too long. He had hardly noticed.

Exasperated, Ann took out the scissors, needle and thread as her hapless husband stood still and powerless, silently obeying his wife's instructions as the room collapsed in a fit of laughter.

Priscilla thought she never loved him more than she did at that moment.

Finally, it was time to go.

Ann went in one car with the bridesmaids as Priscilla stayed behind with her dad.

She held his hand tightly as they walked outside to the Limousine waiting to take them to the church.

I was very emotional as I got into the back of the car with dad.

I was full of doubts, especially after what happened the previous day, but I didn't have the guts to pull back. I didn't want to be on my own.

Maybe it was selfish. I adored my dad and couldn't bear the thought of being without him. We were told [by doctors] the max he had was five years. I knew I was going to lose him at some point.

I didn't want to be left alone. I wanted to have a child. And I wanted it to work, I really did.

I clung to dad that morning. I didn't want to let him go. It felt like it was the end of everything I knew.

Priscilla and Pat sat silently together as the wedding car snaked its way through Dublin's northside to Our Lady of Victories Church in Glasnevin. As the car pulled up outside Pat could sense something was wrong.

'You can pull out of this now, you know,' he told Priscilla as the familiar strains of *Here Comes the Bride* filled the church.

Priscilla was crying, but she shook her head. She smiled up at her dad and walked down the aisle.

She was still crying when Pat handed her over at the altar, but she regained her composure when she looked into her fiancé's eyes.

He was smiling at her, in that confident way of his. Don't worry, he seemed to be saying, I'll look after you from now on.

He looks great, thought Priscilla, even better than me, the cheek of him.

The mercifully swift and pleasant ceremony was delivered by the chief celebrant, Fr Paul Spellman, who had also married Pat and Ann almost 30 years earlier.

Priscilla brushed aside her anxiety, pushed her doubts down to the cold storage room at the pit of her stomach and said, 'I do.'

She kissed her husband and they turned to leave the church with the sound of applause ringing in their ears.

The wedding party made the short journey to the reception at a private golf club near Dublin Airport.

Ann had organised the venue though her cousin, a past captain of the club. The immaculate fairways shimmered under the clear summer sky as the guests cheered the arriving bride and groom.

Everyone was having a great time. Pat called a free round of drinks and the singing soon got underway.

The room was immaculate. Priscilla and Ann had worked hard to ensure everything was perfectly in place for their guests.

There were a few nice extra touches too. Most people in the room had some connection to the bar trade so Priscilla had organised specially made miniature chocolate pints of Guinness for each guest.

As a surprise, Pat arranged for his old friend Paddy Cole, the 'King of the Swingers', and his band to perform for his daughter's big day.

Paddy soon had everyone on the dancefloor.

Pat got up to sing. So did Priscilla. Then all the cousins up from Leitrim.

Her new husband's father was the only blot on the night. He didn't bother to congratulate his son or new daughter-in-law and the occasion clearly failed to lift his mood. The potatoes were too hard. He didn't like having to wear a suit. And then, he announced suddenly, he wouldn't be giving any speech and that was that.

Priscilla was furious.

She had enough to deal with and she wasn't going to let this man, who didn't so much as offer to buy her mam or dad a drink, ruin her wedding day.

Her husband never stood up to his father, but she had a stern word with his brothers.

Eventually, after some persuasion, he managed to force a few words through gritted teeth.

The wedding party began to wind down shortly after 1.30am. Some went back to the Skylon afterwards for a few more drinks.

The newly married couple booked into the hotel for the night so that Priscilla's cousins over from the US could stay in their house, but the bride was exhausted and wanted to go straight to bed.

The day had gone off better than she could have hoped for just a few hours earlier, but she felt sad saying goodnight to Pat and Ann.

Priscilla, now almost 28, was finally leaving her parents and she felt a twinge in her stomach as she climbed into bed for the first time as a married woman.

7

PRISCILLA WAS relieved to finally get on the plane.

The party continued on the day after the wedding. Most of Priscilla's extended family and close friends descended on the Turnstile pub on Blackhorse Avenue, just down the road from Leitrim Lodge.

Only a few of her husband's family turned up, but Priscilla suspected he was happy with this and decided not to mention it.

The next day Pat and Ann organised a barbeque at their house for anyone who had the stomach, and the liver, to keep going.

Priscilla was exhausted by now. She was happy her wedding weekend passed off without incident, but they had an early morning flight to the US and she just wanted to climb into her cot.

The newly-weds flew with Aer Lingus to John F Kennedy Airport in New York, where they had a six-hour stopover before their connecting flight to Orlando, Florida.

They headed to the TWA Flight Centre for lunch, and a few drinks.

'Sure this'll shorten the journey,' Priscilla joked, 'and we can fall asleep on the flight.'

The sun shone through the floor-to-ceiling windows overlooking the runway by Terminal Five as a seemingly endless assembly line of aircraft landed and departed.

The newly married couple laughed and joked as they recalled the last few days that marked the beginning of their new life together.

Priscilla looked down at her ring. It was hard to believe she was finally married.

She still had some doubts, but she really wanted her marriage to work.

The new bride surveyed the scrum of human traffic hurrying to and from what seemed to be every destination on the planet. She felt alive.

This was the type of life she wanted. Love, fun, excitement.

Why shouldn't I have these things, she thought.

By the time the plane touched down in Orlando they were both spent. They'd had a lot to drink over the past three days and it had taken a toll.

Priscilla was a social animal, she loved having the craic, but she wasn't a heavy drinker. And neither was he, most of the time. Five or six pints was usually his limit and he never gravitated towards the top shelf.

It was almost 9pm by the time they arrived at the Clearwater Beach Resort. The hotel, with its sweeping views of the ocean and long sandy beaches, is popular with honeymooners, but the romance of the setting was lost on the exhausted looking Irish couple as they checked in and wearily made their way to their room.

When she woke Priscilla was officially a year older.

They planned to go out for a romantic meal that night to celebrate her 28th birthday, but until then the newly-weds were happy just to soak up the sun and laze the day away and let their batteries recharge.

That evening, as they were getting ready to go out, Priscilla told him to make sure everything was locked away in the safe, but to bring their passports just in case.

They had around $3,000 in cash and traveller's cheques and a small amount on the credit card in case of an emergency.

It was all wedding money. They had very little cash left after the house and the last few weeks had drained what remained of their savings.

Priscilla made a mental note; $3,000 to last two weeks – five days in Florida, five more nights in Vegas and four days in Manhattan before flying home. It would be tight, but she thought they should have just enough to see out the honeymoon.

They arrived at the restaurant, an old-style American grill bar with red booths. Priscilla and her new husband sat across from each other as a waitress arrived to take their order.

They ordered two bottles of Budweiser to begin with. Priscilla was surprised, but also a little flattered, when the girl asked her if she had identification.

'I'm seven months older than he is!' Priscilla laughed as she asked her husband to show the waitress her passport.

'No,' he answered, 'you told me to put it into the safe.'

Priscilla sighed. I told you to bring the passport, she muttered under her breath, but she didn't want to have a row in front of the girl. She ordered a Coke instead.

It was her birthday and the second night of their honeymoon and here she was like a teenager with fizzy drinks while he ordered one beer after another for himself.

Priscilla became more irritated as the evening wore on, but he didn't seem to notice. He also did not offer to make the 10-minute journey back to the hotel room to retrieve his bride's passport.

It was just after midnight when they got back to the hotel. He asked her if she wanted to get a drink at the bar, but Priscilla just wanted to go to bed. She was feeling angry with him as it was. She didn't want drink to add any fuel to the undercurrent of tension she felt simmering between them.

They had a few words. Not a full-scale row, but Priscilla decided it was best to retreat to the room and leave him to it.

When she got back to the room, Priscilla checked the safe. The money was there. And her passport, but not his.

Priscilla grabbed her book and climbed into bed.

About an hour later he came back to the room, but he couldn't get in.

Priscilla was always security conscious and had locked the room from the inside.

She unlocked the door and he walked in.

Priscilla spoke first.

'How come you brought your passport and left mine behind?'

He ignored the question and turned on her.

'Why didn't you fucking stay on with me and have a drink?'

'Because I had to sit drinking Coke on my birthday and the second night of my honeymoon because I didn't have my passport, but you had yours.'

'So you're questioning me?' he challenged her.

'Yes I am.'

Priscilla went to get up from the bed. She leaned over to put her book down on the bedside table when, suddenly, he banged her hard on the shoulder with the open palm of his hand.

Priscilla recoiled in pain and shock. She tried to raise herself up, but he shoved her back down. He stood over her, his face a picture of rage.

'Don't ever fucking question me again.'

The honeymoon was over.

The nightmare had begun.

8

PRISCILLA HARDLY slept a wink, but when her husband woke he acted as if nothing had happened.

She felt sick, nausea rising from her stomach to her throat until she thought she would gag.

Her mind was racing. She wanted to go home there and then, to walk out the door and never turn back. But she was afraid. Afraid of him. Afraid of being on her own. Afraid of being called a failure.

Eventually she mustered the courage to speak.

'I hope you're proud of yourself. How could you hit me? How could you raise your hands to me?'

She thought, and hoped deep down, that he'd say sorry. The drink made me crazy. I don't know what came over me. It'll never happen again. Anything.

But he just brushed her aside.

'I only gave ye a tip. Stop exaggerating.'

'A tip? You really hurt me last night. You hurt me!'

His head was pounding. He clearly didn't want to be having this conversation. He simmered, the hangover just about keeping his blood from boiling over.

But Priscilla wouldn't let it go.

Until he snapped.

'Stop this! Give it up – you're making a mountain out of a fucking molehill!'

Priscilla bit her lip. She was scared and did not want a repeat performance. They were due to go on a cruise for the day, with a candlelit dinner afterwards.

They got ready in silence. Priscilla made sure she had her passport.

She looked at herself in the mirror. She had been looking forward to the cruise ever since she booked the trip with American Holidays on Pearse Street, which now felt like a long time ago.

She looked pale and drained. She reached for her make-up and her hand shook slightly as she put on her mask.

During the cruise, and later at dinner, he continued the act, playing the role of happy husband with an ease that sent a chill through his new bride.

She had a drink to calm her nerves. Then another one. Fuck it, she thought to herself, I'm making up for last night.

But it wouldn't go away, the sick feeling of dread and fear that threatened to overwhelm her.

Shortly after 10pm the drink started talking. Priscilla, by now full of Dutch courage, turned to her new husband: 'You hit me. Nobody raises a hand to me. Don't you ever raise a hand to me again.'

She was repeating herself, she knew, but it felt good to get it out. She felt bolder with every slurred sentence.

He tried to ignore her.

'Will you stop going on about it ...'

But by the time they got back to the room he was ready to erupt.

Priscilla, numbed by the alcohol, failed to read the signs. She kept on.

'Do you not understand? I've never seen anything like this before. You'll never do anything like that to me again, you hear me?'

Finally, he snapped.

'Shut the fuck up about last night!' he screamed in her face.

'You never fucking stop. You're like a dog with a bone. Big fucking deal!'

'It's a big deal to me – I'm the one that married you.'

Then came the insults.

'I fucking married you. Sure who else would marry you? I took you off the shelf.'

The shouting continued, until he could no longer contain the anger.

Her grabbed his bride hard under the arms, digging his nails into her flesh. Priscilla cried out in pain, but he shook her violently and pushed his hand against her throat.

'Do you not get it into your fucking head? I didn't mean to do it!'

Priscilla's courage evaporated.

Now she was very afraid.

She tried to push her way past him towards the door, but he dug his elbow into her side.

He kept digging as she lay on the ground, ignoring her desperate child-like cries for him to stop.

'I want to go home, please let me go home.'

'Ah yeah, home to mammy and daddy! Run home to mammy and daddy! Tell them it's all my fault!'

He looked at her coldly.

'You can't go fucking home. This is it.'

The beating on the third night of our honeymoon lasted around 15 minutes, but it felt like a lifetime.

It felt as if I was trapped in a living nightmare. It didn't seem real.

I knew deep down something was wrong before we got married but I couldn't believe something like this was happening to me.

Who was this person? How did I allow myself to marry someone like this?

My whole world was turned upside down. I just wanted to run away, get back to mam and dad, away from all of this.

On the fourth day of the honeymoon I woke up covered in bruises, but not on my face.

I was very hurt, physically and mentally, but once I was dressed you wouldn't have known I'd been battered a few hours beforehand.

He was always very clever with the beatings. He loved kicking ... he was great with the legs.

9

ON THE fifth morning of the honeymoon Mr Hyde reverted to Dr Jekyl.

Again, it was as if the violence and trauma of the previous night never happened.

But this time Priscilla, with the bruises and pain to remind her, didn't repeat the mistake of challenging him.

She spent the last day in Florida walking around in a daze. Numb.

The events of the past two nights kept flashing in front of her, like lightening reels of a horror film playing over and over in her mind.

Priscilla had never experienced violence or rage like this before. It was as if her husband really hated her. She was terrified he would erupt again.

It was the first week of their honeymoon and Priscilla was already learning to walk on eggshells.

As she retreated into herself, he took on the role of doting husband with gusto.

The threatening language evaporated, as if he had been gripped by a sudden and inexplicable onslaught of Tourette's.

The impeccable manners that attracted her in the early days were back.

He told her he loved her. He put his arm around her and reassured her everything was going to be OK. He opened the door for her, poured her drink, fussed over her. He charmed strangers who found themselves in their company.

A perfect gentleman smiled across at her; the raging bull was gone.

He never once mentioned or made any reference to the late-night bouts of violence. It was as if they never happened.

To anyone who met them they looked just like any ordinary newly married couple enjoying their honeymoon in Las Vegas.

Priscilla was a prolific shopper and Vegas was the perfect place for an injection of retail therapy.

He also loved the high life, despite rarely having any money. The designer clothes, the restaurants and - Priscilla noticed - the bright lights of the casino.

After dinner he'd say: 'Come on, we'll go and throw a few bob on the roulette table.'

It was fun. The two of them drifted around the casinos lapping up the atmosphere, occasionally placing a small bet here and there. Nothing big.

Priscilla tried her best to block the events of the previous nights out of her mind. Because now they seemed to be getting on really well. They laughed, they joked, they ate and drank and caught a couple of shows. They visited Freemont Street; the old part of Vegas famous for the iconic neon signs adorning some of the city's first casinos.

Not a single cross word passed between them.

But sometimes he would leave her, disappearing for up to two and three hours while Priscilla had a lie-in or was browsing in the shops.

'I went for a walk,' he'd say when she asked him where he was.

On their third day in Sin City, Priscilla noticed the money was haemorrhaging. They'd just $500 left in traveller's cheques. All the cash was gone.

They barely had enough money to buy a few presents for Priscilla's nieces and nephews in New York.

Priscilla was worried, but he just shrugged it off. He called Mastercard and arranged for an extra $600 credit.

No problem, he told her, we'll sort it out when we get back.

When they got to Manhattan they checked into Fitzpatrick's on the Upper East Side.

The last four days of the honeymoon were a whirlwind of gatherings with old friends and family.

Many of them were meeting Priscilla's husband for the first time and they were all taken in by the charming barman who seemed so besotted with his new wife.

———

Everyone loved him. He was back to his best and for a while I thought I was going a bit crazy to be honest.

I knew what had happened, it sent a shiver down my spine anytime I thought about it, but I couldn't believe this man, who loved me so much, could act like this and then go back to being this great guy.

I mean, everyone seemed to love him.

Maybe it was me?

Maybe he was under pressure?

Maybe the wedding just got to him?

Maybe his family got to him?

Maybe I shouldn't have been getting on to him?
Maybe I deserved the box?
I'd look down at the bruises.
Sure, they're not that bad.
They're nearly gone now.

———

But the honeymoon within the honeymoon didn't last long.

After the high of New York, his mood appeared to darken again as they boarded the flight home.

'Nothing – I don't want to talk,' he answered gruffly when she asked what was wrong.

Priscilla was already wary of the signs and decided to let it lie.

It was a night flight. He fell asleep shortly after take-off, but Priscilla was wide awake.

As the plane touched down in Dublin, Priscilla felt the storm clouds gathering in her mind.

Pat and Ann were there to meet them at the airport, and then take them for breakfast to hear all the honeymoon news.

'I don't want to go for breakfast,' he said, putting Priscilla on tenterhooks.

Ann noticed the newly-weds were quiet, but she put it down to tiredness.

They stopped at Leitrim Lodge for a cup of tea and a quick catch up and then Ann dropped them to the house.

They walked silently into their new family home.

There was a surprise inside. Pat and Ann had been in earlier and put the heat on. There was milk and bread with some chutney on the table. And a card with a few quid inside to take the sting out of the homecoming.

Priscilla was suddenly overcome with tiredness, and she was back in work the next morning.

'I'm knackered, I'm off to the bed,' she said wearily.

Her husband didn't bother to answer as she climbed the stairs alone.

Part 3

CONTROL

Part 3

10

THEIR new home was tucked inside a small estate of terraced and semi-detached red brick homes not far from the city centre.

The mostly three-bedroom dwellings, and the location, were ideal for a working couple starting off married life, and Priscilla did everything she could to make their new house a home.

Everything in the house was new-ish, but this was mainly thanks to her parents.

Pat had plenty of contacts in the building trade and he managed to secure most of what they needed at cost, including a beautiful navy upholstered three-piece suite. It was rather old fashioned with big round arms, but Priscilla loved it.

Furnishing a new home can place a heavy financial burden on newly married couples, but her husband hardly had to put a hand in his pocket.

Priscilla tried to put the honeymoon to the back of her mind. They'd had a few rows in their first few weeks in the house, but nothing serious.

After the violence, the fear lingered in the back of her mind that he could explode at any time, but Priscilla was determined to try and make her marriage work.

She began to look at the honeymoon differently.

She blamed herself.

She blamed his family.

It must have been down to me.

He has a lot of pressure with his family.

One night, when her parents were visiting, he opened up about his tough upbringing, how his father often took the belt to him.

The poor guy has suffered, she thought.

Money was tight.

Pat and Ann no longer had the guesthouse and the catering company they now operated with Priscilla was struggling.

Pat was too sick to work, and Priscilla was putting in long hours trying to fill in as best she could.

Her father was in and out of hospital all the time. He was undergoing four blood tests a week, at £80 a go, and Priscilla was only drawing a minimum wage from the business to keep costs down.

Her husband was operating a business Pat helped him to set up, but, Priscilla noticed, he never seemed to have any money of his own.

———

We were both working and earning but I seemed to be paying for everything.

He was paid through invoices, so I understood he wasn't guaranteed his wages every week, but he'd rarely pay for anything.

We were living off my wages and this was also covering all the bills; the electricity, the oil, the mortgage ... and the bills just seemed to keep coming.

I remember him saying we should get the bathroom done up, but the bathroom was fine. He just wanted an excuse to re-mortgage the house to clear off his debts.

Anytime I mentioned money he threw it back in my face, made it all my fault.

'Ye had a great fucking honeymoon, didn't ya? I spent thousands on ye,' he'd say.

But it had nothing to do with the honeymoon.

———

Shortly after moving into the house, Priscilla noticed a distinct pattern of behaviour setting in, especially at weekends.

Every Saturday morning he'd get up early and go off to buy The Star newspaper. When he returned, he'd spread the racing pages across the kitchen table and survey the runners and riders for the day.

Then he'd go off to the 'shop' and come back with his pockets stuffed with betting slips.

He never discussed his bets with Priscilla, but she was happy to let him to his routine. It's his way of relaxing, she told herself.

He would have the stereo speaker on so he could listen to the racing while watching football on the television, the SKY remote always perched on one of the big arms on the navy couch.

Priscilla left him to it and spent most of the day upstairs alone.

Most Saturday nights they went out for a meal and a few drinks.

There were occasional rows, but mostly they were like any young couple enjoying themselves on a night out.

Priscilla noticed his mood depended largely on how his day went.

If it was a good day at the races he would be in great form and they'd go out. But when he lost his mood darkened and his wife knew he was best left alone.

Priscilla noticed she was eating more and had put on a good bit of weight.

Food became my best friend, eating became my crutch.

At first the trigger points followed a distinct pattern; the cravings would begin when he'd kick off before he went to work.

Once he was gone, I would order something in; it gave me comfort and a sense of security.

I needed to feel I was going to be okay and that I hadn't done anything wrong.

I needed to feed that feeling of anxiety ... I'd order Chinese, pizza ... I'd be desperate to get as much into me because I felt that [food] was my strength and this would stop the unease welling up inside me.

I'd feel a huge sense of relief when he was gone, and I'd be able to eat what and when I wanted to in peace.

I thought, mentally, the food was giving me strength, but I was piling on weight and then I'd feel anxious and depressed.

Then I'd go on a diet – usually one of those fad diets – and I might lose a couple of pounds, but the next thing I'd be back to square one.

I also believe he didn't want me to lose weight because it was as if he wanted me to feel bad about myself and this gave him more control.

Then I got sick. I got E. coli, I was put on steroids and quickly ballooned in weight.

He didn't cook anything at home that I was able to eat, so I had to rely on take-aways, all the unhealthy stuff.

Food became my companion. I'd get up in the morning and leave the house as quick as I could to avoid any confrontation. Then I'd stop in the garage, and I'd probably have a breakfast roll and a can of Coke. I'd have a bagel later for lunch.

Dad noticed the change in me, and he was worried. He'd struggled with his weight too and he warned me not to end up like him.

I'd say 'yeah, sure I will,' but he didn't know what I was going through.

Eating gave me comfort, and it made me feel as if I was in some sort of control.

But as I piled on the pounds it became more of an addiction and, the bigger I got, the worse I felt about myself.

I didn't realise it at the time, but my confidence was slowly draining away.

11

PRISCILLA ADORED her parents and always dreamed of having a family of her own that would be just as close.

Despite their problems and her fear of her husband's temper, the first two years of the marriage were relatively happy.

Priscilla was mindful of her dad's health, and she thought having a baby would bring them closer as a couple.

In the autumn of 1997, the Graingers got a massive boost when Pat suddenly went into remission. By now he was on 20 steroids a day and was very bloated, but Priscilla thought it was a turning point.

Shortly afterwards Priscilla discovered she was pregnant. It felt as if all her prayers had been answered.

She began feeling unwell the week before the October bank holiday weekend.

On Saturday, when he disappeared off to the bookies, Priscilla went to the local pharmacy and got a pregnancy test.

Two lines appeared.

She called him straight away, her hands trembling with excitement.

'Can you come home – I need you to come home.'

As soon as he came in the door she told him the news.

'I'm pregnant!'

'How do you know?'

'I did a test.'

'Ah, that's great ...'

Priscilla was sitting on the navy sofa. He was perched on one of the big arm rests.

He put his arm around her shoulder and said: 'That's great, I'll chat to you later about it ...'

Then he got up and walked out the door.

I was completely taken aback. Things hadn't been great but there wasn't any physical violence since the honeymoon, and I thought this [pregnancy] would make everything better.

I was over the moon to be pregnant. I was really excited telling him, but after his reaction I felt completely deflated.

It was dark by the time her husband arrived back shortly after 5pm.

He asked Priscilla if she wanted to go out for a drink. He said his sister and her partner would be joining them.

Priscilla didn't feel like going out and knew she wouldn't be drinking for some time, but she agreed.

They broke the news to Pat and Ann the next day.

Priscilla's parents were overjoyed, but a noticeable change had come over her husband.

His mood transformed dramatically from then on. Everyone was happy [about the pregnancy] except him.

The rows got worse and more frequent; it never stopped, one day after another.

I obviously wasn't drinking but he was going out more than ever.

He never liked me being at home on my own. He wanted me to be out, out, out – but all I wanted to do was sit back and relax at home.

He resented that, he wanted to go out, but he didn't have any real friends of his own.

He'd say to me during the week: 'Why don't you take some time off and we'll go out to town for the night, you can drive.' He never suggested getting a taxi.

It wasn't an easy pregnancy. I was very ill in the early stages; I'd have a bucket beside me every morning from 6am to 10am and I'd be very sick. All I wanted was a cup of tea and a digestive biscuit, but he didn't want to know.

It was like he was pretending I wasn't pregnant, and he would get annoyed anytime I spoke about it.

Around this time, I wouldn't say I stopped [caring about him], but I had to look after myself and my baby, I was carrying our child.

I suppose I went into a zone where I was minding myself. I tried not to create any tension because I was afraid something was going to happen and I didn't want to do anything that would lead to a row.

Despite her sickness, Priscilla was excited about being pregnant, but she felt completely alone.

She attended all the pre-natal classes at the National Maternity Hospital in Holles Street on her own. Her husband didn't attend a single class. He also wasn't there when his wife got the first scan of their baby.

Priscilla's health deteriorated as the pregnancy progressed. She was exhausted all the time and tests eventually confirmed she had diabetes.

'Why do you have diabetes,' was all he said when she told him, as if it was just an annoyance.

Priscilla found herself increasingly seeking sanctuary with her parents on their frequent trips down to Leitrim, where they were all due to spend Christmas together.

By now she was heavily pregnant, so much so she thought she was going to have twins. She even found walking difficult.

It was a particularly cold Christmas. Priscilla, her husband and her parents were crammed into the small cottage as the temperatures and patience levels plummeted.

Then the electricity went.

Pat Grainger took control.

'Feck this,' he said, 'we're not staying here in the cold.'

He called Aer Lingus and, within minutes, had arranged flights and a hotel in London. The four left Leitrim on St Stephen's Day and flew out two days later.

Pat, as usual, picked up the tab, but Priscilla's husband just 'moaned and groaned the whole time.'

It was as if, she thought, he resented having to rely on Pat, but he still rarely put his hand in his pocket.

It was around this time Priscilla first became aware that her husband was controlling her financially.

He questioned everything she purchased. And within a few months into the pregnancy, he had taken full control of her wages and all their finances.

During their Christmas trip to London, Priscilla saw a beautiful swinging crib in Harrods which had been reduced to £69.

'I'm not carrying that,' he told her, but Priscilla insisted: 'We'll get it shipped over.'

But as she recalls: 'I got it in the end, but I paid a big price for it. When we came back he never stopped going on and on about it. "A waste of money."'

By April things had gotten considerably worse. He was frequently prone to violent outbursts and Priscilla no longer had money of her own.

She was reduced to having to beg him for a few quid just to get the essentials.

Every household expense was met with an inquisition.

'Where were you?

'What were you spending?

'What did you buy?

'Show me the receipts!

'Why did you leave the heat on?'

Priscilla was doing everything she could to prepare for their new arrival, but by now she felt she couldn't even discuss the baby with him.

'He didn't prepare a room for the baby, or even talk to me about the pregnancy. He was completely out of the picture. It was killing him that someone else was getting the attention.'

On the last Wednesday of March, 35 weeks into the pregnancy, Priscilla asked her husband for £30 to get a few things for the baby.

'What do you mean? What things?'

'Sure I won't know till I get there ...'

'What do you fuckin' mean?'

Priscilla, months of sadness, frustration and anger building up inside her, snapped.

———

The next thing, I don't know what came over me, I said to him: 'I want some money and I want it now! I am going shopping with my mother and I need money now.'

He exploded.

He stormed into the sitting room and kicked a table.

There was a little Duiske [glass] vase on the table; he picked it up in a rage and threw it straight at me – hitting me straight across the stomach.

The vase bounced from my belly onto the ground and smashed into pieces. I didn't know what to do.

He just walked out the door and drove off, leaving me there.

I had to get myself together, my mother was coming around the corner.

I said to myself: 'Stop crying Priscilla, stop crying. If you go to the doctor and they discover he's been beating you you're going to lose the child, they'll end up putting the child in care.'

———

Ann's car pulled up outside and Priscilla got into the front passenger seat.

She didn't say anything, but her mother sensed something was wrong.

She feigned tiredness and they allowed the silent fiction to play out.

Priscilla was on edge. Her heart was racing and she felt the fear rising up in the pit of her stomach, still sore from the impact of the vase. She prayed the baby hadn't been harmed.

It was only a few minutes' drive to Blanchardstown Shopping Centre, but Priscilla was already gripped with anxiety - and terrified of what was waiting for her when she got home.

She spent around £10 on some vests for the baby and a packet of digestive biscuits.

Ann dropped her home shortly before 9pm and Priscilla went straight to bed. She turned off the light when she heard his van pull up outside two hours later.

No words passed between them the next morning. Priscilla quietly climbed out of the bed and went to work.

Shortly after arriving at the office, she suddenly felt a sensation of wetness and doubled over.

'This can't be,' she said to herself, 'I'm only 35 weeks gone.'

Panicked, she shouted over to her dad: 'Get mam on the phone – I think I'm going into labour!'

Her husband happened to drop into the office. Pat shouted to him: 'You're needed.'

'What?'

'Priscilla's not well.'

Priscilla looked at him and spelt it out: 'My waters have broken.'

She rang the hospital and they told her to come straight in.

Priscilla tried not to panic, breathing heavily in and out as she was helped onto a bed in a busy ward.

Her husband was clearly agitated. He kept muttering about how he 'hated fucking hospital food.'

He turned to the wife he'd flung a vase at just hours earlier and said: 'We need to get things sorted now, we need to get things back on track. I know your hormones are probably all over the place …'

———

My hormones weren't all over the place. I told him: 'You know what you did, this is why I'm in here – you fired that vase at me.'

His voice changed. 'Nah, you're fucking mad.'

I knew what he was up to. He was terrified I'd tell the doctors.

He says, 'I'm off, I don't like hospital food' … and he left. He just walked out.

I was left there on my own as they tried to stop me from going into early labour. They injected steroids into the baby's kidneys, liver and heart.

My waters had broken early, and it was from the trauma.

I told a nurse, I told her what he'd done but she just shrugged. It was a cry for help, but it fell on deaf ears. I didn't even know what domestic violence was back then.

Nobody, apart from mam and dad, came near me in the hospital. I was on my own for the night, all sorts of things racing through my head.

I was so close to telling mam and dad about what happened, but dad had a test the following day and I didn't want to worry him. Then I thought: 'How would they manage with me back at the house with a baby and dad sick?'

So I said to myself: 'You've got to put up with this, you've got no choice.'

Even if the nurse had alerted someone to what I told her, I'm not sure what I would have done to be honest.

My big fear was social services taking the baby; the thought of this terrified me.

———

Much to her relief, Priscilla didn't go into early labour and was allowed to go home to rest the following morning.

Pat was very worried about his daughter and wasn't happy with the level of care she received at Holles Street.

He turned to Ann and said: 'Let's get her out to Mount Carmel [Private Hospital].'

Priscilla was admitted on Friday, May 1, 1998, the day of the 'blue flu' when 5,000 members of An Garda Síochána called in sick in a protest over low pay, the first work stoppage in the history of the force.

And, it appeared to Priscilla, her husband was staging a protest of his own. His wife was about to go into labour, but he only seemed interested in how it was all affecting him.

Eventually she told him to go away when he began to regurgitate his rant about 'fucking hospital food'.

After he stormed out Priscilla felt a wave of sadness wash over her.

She felt completely alone, while everywhere around her she saw happy couples, smiling and together.

Priscilla spent three more days in agony until her obstetrician ordered she be brought into the labour ward.

———

The doctor arrived in and said to him: 'Come down here and hold your wife's hand.'

He was behind the bed; he came around and leaned over. I looked at him and said: 'Get away from me – I'm doing this on my own.'

He stepped back straight away.

The doctor said to me: 'Priscilla, I think we'll [C] section you.'

I told him, 'You will not – I was left here for three days, you can get on with it now!'

I remember shouting, 'five more minutes!"

———

Ainie Faith Grainger was born at 8.58am on Sunday, May 3.

Despite the trauma of the previous few days, it was the happiest moment of Priscilla's life.

She gazed into her daughter's beautiful blue eyes and saw only herself looking back.

'It was as if there wasn't an ounce of him in her. She was the image of me; I was so relieved.'

Pat and Ann were told the good news and came in straight away, already besotted with their first, and only, grandchild.

Priscilla was exhausted. She was barely able to speak by the time her husband's family came in to visit at 2.30pm.

He went home for a few hours before returning briefly later that evening. Then he went out for the night on a session.

Priscilla had an infection, which meant she had stay five more days in the hospital with her baby.

When he eventually came to collect his wife and new baby, Priscilla avoided his gaze as she placed Ainie in the back of the car.

They sat in silence as he drove them home to the north side of the city.

12

PRISCILLA prayed Ainie's arrival would herald a fresh beginning for the couple and maybe bring them closer together.

But her hopes were dashed almost as soon as they brought their little girl home for the first time.

She didn't know what it was then, but Priscilla was suffering from post-natal depression. She thought she was feeling down because of the traumatic events leading up to the birth and the agonisingly long labour that followed.

Priscilla felt a close bond with Ainie, but she couldn't explain the terrible sadness that enveloped her; the anxiety, lack of sleep, being completely zapped of energy.

She felt guilty because she thought having a baby was everything she wanted, but Priscilla found herself withdrawing from everybody, even her parents.

The worried new mother tried to explain how she was feeling to her husband, but he didn't want to know.

'Get your fucking act together and cop on; you're over your pregnancy now.'

Priscilla felt worse and worse. At times she felt as if she was losing her mind.

She felt totally rejected. But, even more worryingly, it seemed as though her husband was rejecting Ainie as well.

He rarely did any feeds at the start and kicked up such as fuss when he did that Priscilla couldn't trust him to get the bottle mixture right.

One day she heard him flinging Ainie's bottles across the kitchen counter, roaring in anger as the powder scattered across the floor.

'Stupid, fucking cunt of a thing!'

She stopped asking him to feed the baby.

———

From day one it was obvious he resented Ainie. He was no longer number one, the centre of attention.

Ainie was number one and he couldn't stand it. He took it out on me whenever he could, not necessarily physically – there weren't too many beatings at this point – but the way he looked at me and talked to me was full of violence.

The relationship went downhill. I was nothing to him any longer, it was clear he had zero respect for me.

I almost felt as if Ainie was my safety valve. I used to think, 'well, he won't hit me while I'm holding her' and at times it felt as if she was a shield.

I just wanted us to be like any other family; I'd ask if we could go out somewhere for a walk, for a drive, anything that would feel like some sort of normality. He'd shout at me to 'get out with her – bring her for a walk' ... he couldn't even bring himself to say her name.

I spent most of my time going in and out of shopping centres, Liffey Valley, Blanchardstown ... anywhere I could bring the baby so he could be on his own in the house.

———

Priscilla withdrew into herself more and more.

As her confidence waned, she focused entirely on Ainie, and her baby became the centre of her universe. She poured all her love into her daughter and did her best to compensate for her father's lack of interest.

Priscilla and Ainie slept together, which her husband hated, and he became increasingly jealous of the bond between them.

One day, when Ainie was six weeks old, he refused to look after his daughter, so Priscilla wrapped the baby in a Moses basket and brought her into work.

Her father was in hospital at the time and Priscilla was already under a lot of pressure trying to keep the business above water.

Priscilla knew they were under pressure financially, but he controlled all the money, the mortgage, the bills and most of the household expenses.

She handed her weekly cheque of £360 over to him every Friday and would get £80 back to pay for groceries and anything Ainie needed.

If he did the shopping, they would end up rowing because he bought the cheaper nappies that would leave Ainie with a rash.

Priscilla found herself, whenever she could, hiding any spare cash behind the Sudocrem in the baby's basket.

The house always felt cold, but anytime Priscilla tried to turn on the heat or complained he would shout her down.

The controlling behaviour extended to food. He didn't seem to get much enjoyment from cooking, and his meals rarely extended beyond his staple speciality; mince with carrots, mash potatoes and gravy.

Priscilla would arrive home from work just before 7pm and be told to sit down at the kitchen table.

'I'm not that hungry, I'll eat later on.'

'Eat the fucking dinner or you're not moving from the table; I'm after fucking standing here all day.'

She knew he was gambling; his entire weekend routine centred around the racing and trips to the bookies, but she didn't think it was a major problem.

Until she noticed the bank statements stopped arriving in the post.

At first, she didn't think anything of it. When she mentioned it to him, he just shrugged and said: 'I don't know … I'll give them a ring.'

Eventually, just days after Christmas on December 29, Priscilla decided to call the bank herself.

She froze as the bank official confirmed their mortgage was now £8,500 in arrears. Did she not get the letters?

Priscilla muttered something about the post and said she'd call back. She searched the house top to bottom before she found the stash of warning letters hidden under one of his drawers.

'I needed to see them because I had to prove to myself that I wasn't going mad,' she recalls.

Priscilla was confused. Where was all the money going? He was earning between £500 and £600 a week, on top of the wages she had to hand over. It didn't make any sense.

When he came home that evening she confronted him. Ainie was upstairs having a nap in her cot.

'We're in serious arrears with the mortgage,' she said.

Initially he tried to fob her off, claiming it must be a mistake.

But when she shoved the bank statements into his face he snapped the papers out of her hand.

When Priscilla turned to walk away he hit her hard on the shoulder. She stumbled onto the sofa and he stood over her, his face contorted in rage.

'I fucking warned you about questioning me.'

She begged him to stop but he was on top of her, pinching her and shouting in anger.

He didn't hit her in the face or anywhere where a bruise would be visible, but Priscilla was convinced he would kill her if he thought he could get away with it.

For the first time since they got married, Priscilla decided she had to get out.

———

I was terrified, and not just for me.

I felt I had no choice; what was I going to do, leave a child with no mother?

I decided to leave that night. After the eruption, he gave me the silent treatment and then muttered something about going out for a drink with his brother.

This was my chance. He left at around 8pm and I started to organise myself.

Then I noticed the car insurance was out of date on the 30th and it was too late to call the PMPA [insurance company].

I packed up the car. I gathered Ainie's things and a few of my bits. I remember it was freezing cold, so I put two layers of clothing on Ainie and a double nappy on her. I put two hot water bottles in the car.

I knew I had a window until around 1am when he'd be back, 2am at the latest, so everything had to be ready by then.

I had everything packed in the boot. Ainie's pram, the bags, everything we'd need for a few days.

I knew he wouldn't have looked in my car [on the way back from the pub] so I put a black sack up the window inside to keep the cold out. The hot water bottles were in the back.

I went back inside and tidied the house and made sure everything was normal, left a few of Ainie's toys scattered around and the dirty bottle from her night feed. Then I went to bed.

I knew he'd be locked when he came in and would go straight to bed in the back room, which he usually did when he was drunk.

Sure enough, he eventually came in the door at around 2am and went straight into the back room.

I was delighted ... then I thought how strange it was to be delighted to be smuggling your child out of your own home in the middle of a freezing winter night.

I got dressed, just had to throw my clothes on over my night gear. Everything was in the car, everything was ready, I had nothing else to do, the phone was charged.

I got Ainie and put her into the car in between the hot water bottles.

I turned the ignition and drove slowly up the Navan Road with tears in my eyes.

By now it was half three in the morning.

Dublin's streets were deserted as Priscilla drove to the insurance company's offices on Wolfe Tone Street.

She pushed an envelope under the door with cash for half the insurance that expired at midnight, along with a note urging them to renew the policy with a promise that the balance would be paid the next week.

Priscilla drove west out of the city centre in the direction of Leitrim and to the sanctuary of her parents.

As morning dawned, Priscilla pulled over to give Ainie a bottle. She left the engine running to keep them warm.

She called her mother when they were close to the cottage.

'Mam, I've left him ...'

Ann and Pat were waiting for them at the gate when Priscilla pulled up in the car.

Her mother carried Ainie inside as Pat cloaked his big arms around his daughter.

Despite everything, she wasn't ready to tell her father about the violence.

'Dad, it's all down to gambling – he's going to destroy me,' she said as she collapsed into her father's embrace.

13

BACK IN her parents' safe house, Priscilla cried tears of relief and regret as she grieved over the disintegration of her marriage.

'I didn't sign up for this life,' she said feeling sorry for herself, and for her daughter.

Pat was appalled at his son-in-law's behaviour, even without knowing the problem extended far beyond the gambling.

'No one did, and no-one's asking you to. If you want to leave [for good], we'll deal with it,' he assured her.

But back in Dublin, Priscilla's husband didn't even know his wife and daughter had left. It was midday – more than four hours after Priscilla and Ainie arrived at the cottage – before he noticed they were not in the house.

Eventually the call came.

'You walked out? How fucking dare you walk out on me,' he shouted down the phone.

'Bring that child back here.'

Priscilla shivered, but with her mam and dad beside her she managed to keep it together.

'Listen, your bullying doesn't work anymore. I'm not going back; I'm not prepared to put up with you and your financial and emotional abuse ...'

Priscilla didn't mention the violence in front of her parents.

'You never leave me alone and we're up to our necks in debt and you're still at this.'

She felt her hands shake as she put down the phone.

A short time later the phone rang again.

It was him, but the anger had subsided. Now he just sounded desperate.

'If you don't come back I'm gonna get a rope and hang myself.'

Then, just minutes after threatening his wife, he began to beg.

'I promise I'll get my life together. I won't gamble anymore. We'll get things sorted - I'll get the debt sorted.'

Priscilla hadn't slept a wink and could feel herself starting to wilt.

'Just leave me alone,' she said as she lowered the phone and broke down crying.

—————

This was the beginning of what would become a pattern; when the shouting and the bullying wasn't working, he'd play on my emotions.

First the shouting and the threats. When that doesn't work, he threatens to kill himself.

It was like a switch he could turn on and off whenever he wanted. He could make me go from being terrified of him to actually feeling sorry for him, that it was somehow all my fault.

Looking back now I can see it was all part of his way of controlling me; the relationship, the finances, the food, what I wore, what Ainie was doing ... but at the time, no matter how bad things got, there was always that thought at the back of my mind that it was my fault too.

And I still wanted to believe he could change and that I could save our marriage.

———

The next morning was the first day of the last year of the millennium.

Priscilla hoped the New Year would mark a new beginning for her and Ainie, but she was afraid of what the future would hold.

Her parents would help, of course, but the thought of being a single mother scared her.

The phone calls kept coming, and Priscilla felt her resolve weaken.

Pat came into her room to check on her.

He was worried about his daughter falling into serious debt. Pat advised her to meet her husband at a 'neutral playing field' to try and gauge the extent of his gambling problem.

Eventually, she agreed to meet him halfway in Virginia, county Cavan, at midday.

Priscilla was taken aback by his appearance and body language.

The arrogant swagger was gone. His eyes were dark and hooded and full of remorse.

Priscilla steeled herself.

'I'm not going back,' she told him.

'This is not a marriage. This is not an environment to bring up a child – I don't feel safe anymore.'

He apologised and begged her not to leave. Then he burst out crying. 'Please, give it another go. I'll change,' he pleaded.

'I'm not going to lose you for the sake of gambling, for the sake of drink. I'm going to get it sorted.'

Eventually, after more than two hours, Priscilla told him she needed more time to think and walked back to her car.

She felt drained but empowered. This was the first time in the marriage she had really stood up to him.

When she arrived back at the cottage, Ann and Pat said they'd support her, whatever she decided.

Priscilla stayed for two more days before she packed up Ainie and headed back to Dublin.

14

PRISCILLA DROVE home full of hope.

He promised to go to counselling for the gambling. They'd get to the bottom of their financial problems together. No more shouting, no more threats. It would be a whole new start.

He was waiting for them at the doorway when Priscilla turned the car into the driveway.

He seemed different, lighter somehow. He took their bags and made a fuss over Ainie.

The dinner was on.

'Bloody mincemeat again,' Priscilla muttered to herself as she caught the familiar waft emanating from the kitchen.

But she didn't mind; he was trying to make an effort and Priscilla appreciated it.

He slept in the back bedroom that night. To give her some space, he said.

Priscilla went back to work the next morning and by the time she returned home Mr Hyde was back in character.

He wasn't angry or abusive, just stone cold towards his wife and daughter.

Priscilla was shocked at the sudden mood change.

In the space of a few days, he'd gone from attacking and threatening his wife to breaking down in tears and begging for her forgiveness. Then, literally overnight, from acting like a perfect husband to a perfect stranger who behaved as if he wanted to be a million miles away from them.

She knew then it had all been a ploy to get them back.

———

It was all just an act; he did what he had to do to get us back and be in control again. But it was one hell of a performance – he had me fooled hook, line and sinker.

I remember then feeling very afraid, for me and for Ainie. I knew I was living with a sociopath, someone who could turn from being a complete charmer to violence in a matter of seconds.

I remember saying to myself: 'I've made a massive mistake – I'm not going to get out of here.'

I felt trapped. I thought my only responsibility now was to my baby.

———

The coldness continued for the next nine months. There were few rows and no physical violence, but Priscilla was more than often walking on eggshells around him. She decided to stay out of his way as much as possible and just focus on Ainie.

They spent a lot of time with Pat and Ann and most weekends down at Cully Cottage where Priscilla's parents doted on their only grandchild.

They went on long walks around Garadice Lough, one of Pat's most treasured places where Priscilla could temporarily escape the chill of her marriage troubles.

Thankfully, Ainie was a very happy baby and seemed oblivious to her father's coldness and her mother's deepening anxiety. He rarely accompanied them to Leitrim and that suited Priscilla fine. At least she could feel free at the weekend.

Back in Dublin, he was firmly in control of the finances and assured Priscilla the mortgage payments were back on track.

Priscilla didn't trust him, but she didn't see any more white letters coming through the door and was afraid of provoking him again.

He still had his Saturday betting routine and there was no mention of counselling since their New Year's Day summit in Cavan, but Priscilla allowed herself to believe they were, financially at least, in a better place.

Aside from work, Ainie became her sole occupation. Her husband clearly resented their relationship and silently fumed that he was no longer the centre of attention.

He told Priscilla to move the baby's cot out of their bedroom into the nursery, but she refused.

It was as if there was a sort of unspoken agreement between us; he controlled the money and went about his everyday business like an angry drill sergeant while I had Ainie and most of the weekends with mam and dad.

There was no violence, but it was pure financial and emotional abuse.

It sounds terrible; Ainie was only a baby, but she was like a shield.

He wouldn't hit me when I had her and I clung to her.

Despite their financial problems, he assured Priscilla everything was back on track.

They discussed going on holiday, their first with Ainie as a little family. He suggested Disneyland in California.

Priscilla was taken aback; she wasn't thinking of anything that extravagant, but he seemed in good form for the first time in ages and their first holiday with the baby could be just what they needed to bond.

Priscilla worried about the cost, but he had a solution; re-mortgage the house, pay off the arrears and keep some left over to pay for the holiday.

Feck it, she thought. Disneyland seemed like a dream distraction from their dreary existence.

I was excited and nervous at the same time.

He was in good form to begin with, but then he'd get that look in his eye and I'd begin to worry.

It was all highs and lows; he could blow hot and cold within a few minutes.

I was excited for Ainie and during the day we'd have a great time together.

But by evening it felt like he was a different person. He just wanted to be on his own, down in the bar, away from us.

So we'd stay in the room, sometimes I'd put Ainie into the buggy and take for her a walk around the hotel.

The smallest thing seemed to put him in bad humour and sometimes he'd just ignore us, not saying anything at all for up to an hour.

But I wanted to make the best of it and tried to put it out of my mind.

I wanted this to be a real family holiday, for Ainie especially, but also to finally have some good memories to cherish.

———

One evening as Priscilla was relaxing before dinner, he announced he was going down to the bar for a drink.

Priscilla was quietly relieved. She'd spend a few quiet moments with Ainie before getting ready without him pacing up and down giving out about the time.

He'd been moody for most of the day and Priscilla was happy to get him out of her hair for a while.

She said she'd meet him in the bar at 7pm. But as she was about to leave, he was suddenly back in the room and – Priscilla quickly clocked with alarm – in a foul mood.

'I'm almost ready,' she told him, 'the buggy is loaded.'

'I'm not going out, I've had enough,' he shot back.

Priscilla's heart slumped. Stuck in a confined room when he was in this mood was the last place she wanted to be.

'Ah come on,' she tried to cajole him. 'It's a beautiful night and we're in California. I'm dressed up and the baby is ready to go. Can we ...'

Suddenly he was on top of her.

'Fuck you – I said we're not going down!

'You do as I say,' he shouted as he pushed Priscilla against the wall beside the bed.

'For God's sake, please!' she pleaded as he grabbed her on the ground, alternatively punching and pinching his wife.

She saw the anger in his eyes and smelled the stale drink on his breath as the blows landed.

Priscilla closed her eyes and prayed it would pass quickly and that Ainie, asleep in the buggy, would not wake or witness any of it.

Mercifully, it didn't last long this time. The rage subsided and he climbed onto the bed before passing out.

Priscilla waited until the snoring started and then helped herself up. She felt pains all over her body and had to stop herself from crying out loud.

She went into the bathroom and tried to wipe the tears from her eyes and the make-up smeared across her face.

Quietly, she picked up the baby and cradled her in her arms.

'It's going to be ok,' she whispered over and over, to Ainie and probably herself.

Priscilla went outside to the balcony and tried to calm herself, but the violence and the strain and stress of the last few months overwhelmed her. She sat slumped in the corner crying silently but uncontrollably.

What in God's name am I going to do?

How am I going to get through this?

How can I keep Ainie safe?

Should I go to the police?

Would they even believe me?

Just like the honeymoon, when her husband came through the following morning he acted as if nothing had happened.

She was incredulous. How was he able to switch on and off like that?

'I just had a bit of a mad one last night,' he said, shrugging off his wife's version of events.

'Nah, you're mad,' he told her.

'It was only a tip.'

For the rest of the week he was the model husband and father, cracking jokes and charming anyone that came into their company.

Priscilla bit her lip and kept Ainie close.

She was beginning to understand the drill by now.

15

THE DISNEYLAND nightmare would be the last time Priscilla would suffer a violent assault at the hands of her husband for a few years.

By now she understood this wasn't because he felt any guilt or remorse for his actions, only that he felt secure and in control of all aspects of her life.

When people think of domestic abuse the first thing that usually comes to mind is physical or verbal violence. But while many cases of domestic abuse do not involve violence, international studies show financial abuse occurs in almost every domestic abuse case.

By the year 2000, while Priscilla did not yet even completely comprehend the term domestic violence, she understood ceding control of her money and her independence greatly diminished the chances of getting a physical beating.

She knew he was still gambling and guessed their financial situation wasn't as rosy as he portrayed, but she knew she had to play the game to survive.

Priscilla tried to put aside her own unhappiness, fears and worries and instead invested all her love and whatever positive energy she possessed in her daughter.

It was an intense, symbiotic relationship, something that has remained to this day.

Even when she was a toddler, Ainie understood Priscilla was her protector, even though she didn't realise then she was fulfilling the same role in many ways for her mother.

Her father was different. He was more distant, a stern and forbidding figure she had to be wary of, without yet understanding why.

Up until late 2000 Priscilla's husband ran his own company, but he struggled to get the business off the ground.

He wanted to get a taxi licence, but he didn't have the money or even his own car.

Again, Pat came to the rescue. Despite his misgivings about his son-in-law, Pat believed his problems stemmed solely from gambling. He wasn't aware of the abuse or occasional bouts of violence, which Priscilla kept from him.

Pat told him to sell his van, loaned him some money and then sold him his own car on the cheap to get him started.

Almost as soon as her husband's taxi was on the road, Priscilla noticed a marked change in his mood and behaviour.

———

All of a sudden he was in great form. He was anywhere and everywhere; it was like he had been given wings; he was free.

He'd start at seven in the evening and didn't finish until seven in the morning.

He had money, a lot more than before; he was making £1,500 some weeks, but I never saw any of it.

I was paid about a third of this from the business, but I didn't see much of my own money either.

My wages at the time were £508 a week and he'd give me back £130, and this was what kept the house going ... groceries, nappies, the lot.

The rest was supposed to have been lodged for the mortgage and utility bills as, you know, my share towards it. But I was covering the lot – he cleaned me out and I could never question what he was doing with the taxi money.

It was obvious he was gambling a lot, but I didn't know the extent of it.

He now had access to cash – lots of it – and he stopped using the credit cards to place bets.

It was like we were living in parallel universes. He'd mind Ainie at home during the day while I was at work. I'd come in at 6.30pm and he'd be out the door at seven.

We were like ships in the night.

———

Despite enjoying his new-found freedom, he still kept a close watch on Priscilla.

He didn't like anyone calling to the house, especially when he wasn't there. He wanted to know who she was talking to and what they were talking about.

He didn't want Priscilla's friends calling over, even female ones.

Despite everything they had done for him, he also didn't like Ann or Pat coming around. He saw threats to his dominance everywhere.

Sometimes when Priscilla was at home alone with Ainie at night she would see his taxi prowling by the house, checking to see if there was another car in the driveway.

During the fleeting half hour their lives intersected each evening he would question her relentlessly.

Who did she meet in work?

Where did she go to do the shopping?

What did she have to eat?

How much did she spend?

Eventually, after two years of being worn down under constant surveillance and with only enough money to pay for food and some clothes for Ainie, Priscilla told him she'd had enough.

She was afraid he'd explode again but was taken aback when he agreed to attend marriage counselling.

If he would only open up and communicate with me, we might be able to make things work, she thought to herself.

Priscilla did some research, found a reputable psychotherapist and made an appointment.

But she quickly realised she was doing all the running. He just grunted and seemed to play along as if it was some annoying game. And once the sessions began it soon became apparent to Priscilla that he was only using the counselling as a ploy to stop her from leaving again.

When Priscilla brought up his controlling behaviour, the gambling, the violence, he simply denied everything.

'She's mad ... I never touched her,' he told the counsellor with a straight face.

16

THEY CONTINUED to go to counselling, but Priscilla no longer held out much hope for the marriage.

As they went through the motions, he became even more distant, emotionally and literally. He worked the streets at night and Priscilla did her best to avoid him during the day.

But although their relationship was falling apart, Priscilla was otherwise relatively content. The business was picking up, the beatings had stopped, and her dad's health continued to improve.

And there was Ainie, her little jewel and the one really great thing that had come out of an otherwise miserable marriage.

Priscilla began to view her husband more with distain, her fear gradually turning to disgust.

She felt sad, and at times a little guilty, over the failure of the marriage, but she was even more concerned about his reluctance to bond with their daughter.

Despite the dark atmosphere in the house she grew up in, Ainie was a happy child who charmed anyone who came into contact with her. But her father remained distant and brooding. To Priscilla it appeared as if he resented the little interloper who commandeered all the attention away from him and his needs.

Priscilla also noticed, with alarm, that he seemed to be getting more and more irate around his daughter, sometimes for no apparent reason. She knew all too well what it was like to feel the brunt of that rage.

One day, when Ainie was just two, she came into the living room happily clutching a bottle of 7Up before distractedly squirting some of the soft drink onto the carpet.

Her father let out a roar at the terrified toddler and slapped her on the hand.

The whole exchange took just a split second, but Priscilla felt as if time stood still as she saw her baby being physically assaulted by her abuser.

Fuelled with a mother's rage, Priscilla grabbed him by the back and punched him in the neck with all the force she could muster.

He stumbled backwards in shock, but before he could react Priscilla had scooped Ainie up in her arms and stood over him. For a fleeting moment the tables had turned, and he stayed silent as, for once, his wife was in control.

'Don't you ever lay your hand on her again,' she spat, edging closer to him.

'Get out of my face, ya scumbag ya.'

He stormed out the door as Priscilla cradled her cub in her arms. But this time she was the protector. After years of mental, and at times physical torture, mother bear finally bared her teeth and left her abuser in no doubt that she would die before letting him hurt the thing she loved most in the world.

———

I was shaking, but to be honest I felt great. It was the first time I really stood up to him and I remember the feeling of power that came with the rage when I saw him slap Ainie.

After that he became even more distant, sometimes he completely ignored me – it was like he was pretending I wasn't there, like I was worthless.

He started acting strangely around Ainie when I was around, almost as if he was trying to taunt her because he knew he couldn't hit her or raise his voice at her while I was there.

'Mammy's little girl, aren't ye,' he'd say.

Other times he behaved more like a jealous little brother competing for attention than a father.

'Who's the best, mammy or daddy ...'

As her husband retreated and became more distant, Priscilla noticed he was spending more and more time on his phone.

He never took calls in front of Priscilla and sometimes would take off for days at a time.

She noticed a pattern developing around the big events on the racing calendar. He'd take a week off in March for Cheltenham, another week at Easter for Fairyhouse and Punchestown in April. He would usually work around the Leopardstown festival at Christmas because the money was good, but Priscilla rarely saw him.

As time went on she became convinced he was having an affair.

One evening, on a rare occasion when he left his phone down, Priscilla heard a flurry of texts coming through.

She picked up the Nokia handset and saw a message from 'Mary'.

'Hi – are you free tonight?'

It wasn't proof of infidelity, but Priscilla never heard any mention of a Mary before. When she questioned him about it, he snapped the phone out of her hand and told his wife to mind her own business.

Priscilla was furious, but also still afraid of pushing him over the edge.

From then on, he always kept his phone well hidden. He became even more taciturn when it came to the other life he appeared to be living at night. Sometimes he was away for days at a time without Priscilla even knowing where he was.

Despite his growing detachment, he still kept an iron grip on the family finances and Priscilla struggled to keep enough aside for food and clothes for herself and Ainie.

While she was reduced to searching for end-of-date food bargains in Tesco, he was always dressed head to toe in designer gear. Tommy Hilfiger, Calvin Klein and M&S were his favourites.

Priscilla loved the thought of one day having a big family, but this dream evaporated as her marriage descended into a chaos of abuse and coercive control.

So she was quite taken aback when one day he casually suggested they should try for more children. It had been a long time since they'd even been intimate, so Priscilla was naturally suspicious.

But he began to talk her around. Their finances were in a much better state, he assured her. Maybe it was a good time to move to a bigger house. It would be like a whole new start.

He kept chipping away at Priscilla and, eventually, she relented. The catering business was going well and although she only got to keep a portion of her wages, she allowed herself to believe they had turned a corner, financially at least.

She wanted to stay near her mam and dad, so they started looking at properties nearby. They narrowed it down to one particular property on the Navan Road, just a stone's throw away from Pat and Ann's house, and in April 2005 they put in an offer, which was accepted.

But something was niggling away at Priscilla. She couldn't square her husband's behaviour towards Ainie with this new-found desire to have a bigger family.

It was obvious he didn't even want to be around his wife and child unless it suited his own needs and Priscilla soon realised it was all about the money. When he ran out of money or fell into debt, her husband often tried to loan his way out of trouble, pushing his debt problems further on the long finger.

It was around this time that Pat's health took a turn for the worse. He had been doing pretty well for a few years on his Predsoine medication and Priscilla and Ann were distraught when he came out of remission.

Priscilla knew if she legally separated from her husband they would have to sell the house and he would be entitled to half.

But that wasn't all. Because of her father's health and age, Priscilla's name was on the deeds of her parents' house on the Navan Road and the cottage in Leitrim. Now she feared her husband would go after the whole lot.

A large portion of her parents' income went on Pat's medical and hospital bills. And here they spared no expense; from the Wilmour Eye Clinic in Baltimore, White Plains Hospital in New York, University

Hospital Aintree in Liverpool and, recalls Priscilla, 'every hospital in Dublin bar the maternities'.

All their remaining wealth was tied up in the properties, which her husband had a legal claim over.

Priscilla's fears about her husband's motives were heightened by further signs he was having an affair.

In early February 2006 he casually mentioned he was going away for the weekend 'on a job' with a taxi pal he'd never even mentioned before.

Priscilla also noted the change in his behaviour; the cockiness, the new clothes, the way she sometimes caught him looking at her, his mouth slightly upturned in a grimace.

She felt sick to the stomach.

Priscila didn't have any proof, but instinctively she believed he was trying to manipulate her and Pat's illness to carve out a financial nest egg for himself and whatever new life he was planning.

She withdrew the offer on the house, blaming her father's health.

Priscilla knew her husband was living a double life she knew nothing about but felt powerless to act.

But later that month the shocking murder of a young mother would have a profound effect on Priscilla and set in chain a series of event that would change her and Ainie's lives forever.

17

ON FEBRUARY 28, 2006, Siobhan McLaughlin was found dead in a locked bedroom of her home in the affluent Dublin suburb of Goatstown.

Initially it looked as if Siobhan had tragically taken her own life.

But within hours of her death, gardai and Siobhan's family were certain she had been murdered. It soon emerged the striking blonde mother and successful businesswoman had been strangled to death with a vacuum cleaner flex.

Siobhan's sister Niamh found her in the upstairs bedroom at 9.30am after she let herself into the house with her own key. Her three-year-old nephew, Siobhan's son Daniel, was found walking around the house on his own.

Priscilla and Siobhan were childhood friends. Born just weeks apart, they grew up together in county Meath.

The McLaughlins and Graingers were very close. Priscilla was an only child and loved the warm chaos of Siobhan's house where she spent many afternoons with her best friend and her seven siblings; Brighid, Deirdre, Aisling, Caroline, Ann Marie, Niamh and Owen.

Pat and Ann were close friends of Siobhan's parents, Owen and Deirdre, and they regarded each other's children almost as their own.

Priscilla first met Siobhan when she was nine, and they quickly became inseparable.

They did everything together; the summer jobs picking strawberries, playing camogie, going to the local disco, meeting boys for the first time.

One time, when she was just 12, Siobhan took her mother's car and drove it around the garden as Priscilla looked on with a mixture of horror and admiration. Siobhan was grounded for a week, but the punishment did nothing to keep her spirit in check.

'She was so full of life, I can't tell you how full of life she was,' Siobhan's mother Deirdre recalls.

'Priscilla and Siobhan had this fantastic energy; if there was a wall they'd knock it down to get over it.'

With Siobhan around there was always excitement and Priscilla was happy to follow her effervescent friend, who also became her protector.

While Siobhan mostly led the way, she and Priscilla were alike in many ways. They were both, in Priscilla's words, 'bould', free spirited and they shared the same entrepreneurial spirit. Both would end up working in hospitality; Siobhan eventually opening a beautiful guesthouse, The Hotel Salvia in Majorca, where she moved with her husband Brian Kearney and Daniel three years before she was brutally murdered.

Kearney was interviewed by gardai a few days after his wife's body was found in their home.

Almost three months later he was arrested and questioned by investigating officers for eight hours, but then released without charge.

Priscilla was in Temple Street children's hospital with Ainie when she got the phone call. Ainie had been hit with a basketball in the playground. She wasn't seriously injured but Priscilla didn't want to take any chances and was walking into the hospital with her daughter when her mobile rang.

Her friend Siobhan was dead, possibly murdered.

Priscilla felt the ground shift underneath her. Although she hadn't spoken to Siobhan that much since they both got married, the Graingers and McLaughlins remained close. Priscilla thanked her friend for the call, hung up and immediately called Siobhan's mother.

Priscilla had never warmed to Kearney and couldn't understand what her vivacious friend saw in him.

He was more than 10 years older than her, was devoid of charisma and, to Priscilla, seemed cold and calculating.

Siobhan was an incredibly attractive, intelligent woman. It was obvious why he was attracted to her, but I couldn't for the life of me understand what she saw in him.

In the early days of my own relationship, Siobhan and Kearney were living out in Dalkey and one day we met them for a while out there.

It was like Siobhan was a different person.

The whole time she barely spoke two words and when we were going, she gave me a big hug and I could see tears in her eyes.

He was so rude – he kept saying 'c'mon, c'mon' to Siobhan – trying to get her home.

I tried to connect [with Siobhan] when I was getting married.

Deirdre and Owenie came to the wedding and I hoped deep down that she would connect with me, but I knew it wasn't her fault [that she didn't].

It was him.

———

By the time Siobhan was murdered Priscilla understood only too well what it felt like to come under someone else's spell. To lose almost all sense of who you are under the grip of someone who controlled every aspect of your life.

That evening, after getting Ainie checked out, Priscilla went home and sat alone in the kitchen.

Her husband had left for work, or whatever other life he was leading when he walked out the door every evening.

———

I remember sitting in the kitchen crying.

I went and got the Evening Herald, came back and sat at the table and tried to breathe in slowly.

Siobhan was my best friend, now she'd been murdered.

I allowed my friendship to be ruined because of my husband.

And then it dawned on me; we're in the same situation.

I remember that night thinking: 'If I don't get out of this marriage I'm going to end up in a grave just like Siobhan.'

But where was I going to go?

My father was seriously ill and was probably going to die.

We were in serious debt and the business was starting to struggle.

Where could I go? Where was I going to bring my seven-year-old child?

I felt trapped, but I knew I had to find a way out before it was too late.

18

A PLAN BEGAN to form in Priscilla's head.

She knew she needed proof of his infidelity. Easier said than done, but there could be no wiggle room, no way out. She needed to catch her husband in the act.

He was planning a few days away at the Galway Races in early August. The 2006 event, with the infamous Fianna Fáil tent and multi-millionaire developers competing for helicopter landing spaces in the fields around Ballybrit, would mark one of the last grand hurrahs of the Celtic Tiger.

Priscilla saw her chance. They'd been to the Galway Races with her parents in the past, so after he left for the weekend with a friend, she called him and casually suggested coming down to join him for a night.

He was a little hesitant at first, but then he agreed.

Priscilla got off the phone and immediately booked a flight to Galway. She went upstairs and grabbed a spare set of car keys he didn't know she had and packed her bag.

She told him she was getting a later flight and by the time she arrived at the hotel the following morning he had already left for the races.

Priscilla dropped her bag in the room and made straight for his car.

Inside, she found two mobile phones, one of which she had never seen before. She turned on the unfamiliar

Pat and Ann Grainger   *Pat and Priscilla Grainger*

Priscilla on her confirmation day   *Ainie*

Ainie

Pat and Ainie

Priscilla and Ainie

Pat Grainger

Pat and Ann on holiday in La Cala

Ann Grainger

Doting grandad Pat and Ainie

Ann and Ainie in Leitrim

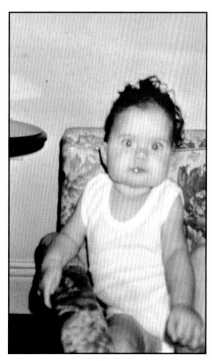

Baby Ainie

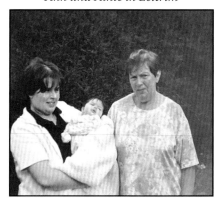

Priscilla, Ainie and Ann

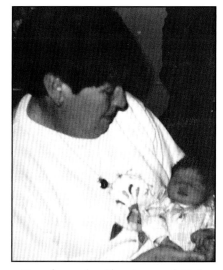

Proud grandmother Ann and Ainie

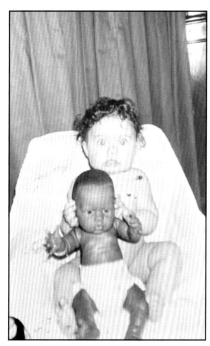

Ainie with her favourite doll 'Kizzy'

Pat, and Ann on Priscilla's 21st

Ann and Priscilla on Priscilla's wedding day

Pat, Ann and Priscilla

Ainie on her christening day

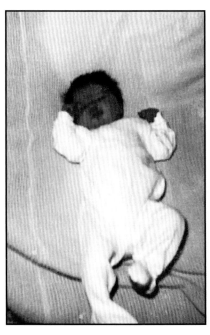

Baby Ainie

Priscilla and Ainie

Pat and Ann's pub in Ballybough

Priscilla and Ainie at the Mansion House
after meeting the former Lord Mayor, Paul McAuliffe

*Ann, Priscilla and Ainie on
her 18th birthday*

*Priscilla and Ainie on
her 18th birthday*

Ainie, Ann and Priscilla on her 50th birthday

Ainie and Priscilla

Priscilla and Ainie

Priscilla and Ainie in Disneyland

Pat and Ann

Ainie on her communion day

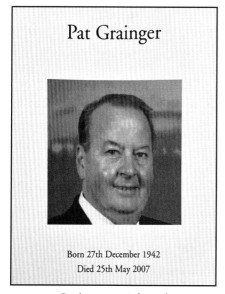

Pat's memorial card

Priscilla and Ainie on her communion day

Ainie addresses the Cambridge Students' Union

Ainie as a baby

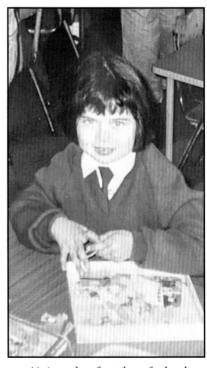

Ainie on her first day of school

handset, scrolled through the messages and then saw the texts. There was nothing expressly intimate, mostly perfunctory exchanges.

'See you in the car park at 11am.'

'See you in town.'

'Tell [his friend] I'll see him at the [location].'

Then she saw from the texts that he had checked into another hotel in the city.

Her heart sunk. She knew something was going on and it hardly came as a surprise, but the confirmation was still crushing.

Priscilla looked at the time; she had to move quickly now. She took photographs of the texts and meticulously left everything in the car exactly as she found it and went back to her room to freshen up.

He arrived back shortly afterwards, surprised she was down so early, but he didn't give anything away.

'Ah, you're here, how's things?'

'Ah grand,' she replied, doing her best to avoid his gaze.

They went out for a meal that night and then to the races the following morning. After a while he told Priscilla he was going to place a bet and left her at the racetrack.

A half hour passed, then 45 minutes.

Priscilla tried her husband's phone, but it went straight to his voicemail.

An hour passed, then two.

Finally, after countless calls, he returned two and a half hours later.

Priscilla guessed where he'd been and struggled to keep her mask from slipping.

He looked flustered.

'Where the bloody hell were you?'

'I came back and you weren't here,' he lied.

'Absolutely no way – I've been sitting here like a thick for two and a half hours – you left me sitting here on my own.'

'No, I didn't,' he insisted, his voice rising. 'I came back and you weren't here.'

Priscilla knew it was pointless pushing it any further and, despite her anger, she was still afraid of him. She dreaded the thought of spending another night in a hotel room with him in a drunken rage.

Instead, she decided to use his vanishing act to her advantage.

He was trying to calm her, so she let it drop and played stupid.

'Ah well, we must have kept missing each other … sure what about it … let's enjoy the night.'

He bought her more drink. Priscilla didn't drink shorts, just Heineken, and he was going to the bar every few minutes for more rounds. When he was gone Priscilla spilled the drink from her glass and pretended to slur her words a bit when he came back from the bar.

———

I had some of the evidence I came for. I was gutted but I was afraid he'd erupt again when we got back to the room, so I played along.

He was going to the bar and back like a yo yo and I had to be careful not to let him know I was onto him.

Thankfully the rest of the night went without incident. He passed out in the hotel room, but I couldn't sleep a wink.

I knew the marriage was over, but I still didn't know what his plan was, and I needed to build up my evidence.

I was disgusted, disgusted, disgusted … but I couldn't do anything.

I knew dad didn't have very long. A few days later I got legal advice and they told me what I didn't want to hear; if I took any form of proceedings against him everything would be sold. Bottom line.

Everything would be gone; the catering business because dad wouldn't be there, the properties too.

I knew he didn't care about us. He was whoring around, laughing at me behind my back, living the high life while I'm working to the bone and struggling to make ends meet.

The country was staring into a recession, and it was as if he was laughing at me all the way.

I knew I had to get out, but I was trapped. He seemed to be holding all the cards.

19

Friday, May 25, 2007

PRISCILLA WOKE shortly before 6am and felt her stomach churn.

She took a deep breath and quietly climbed out of the bed, putting on a pair of tracksuit bottoms and a loose-fitting top as the RTÉ News headlines broke the morning silence.

It was a beautiful blue-sky day, but the storm clouds of recession were looming on the horizon just a day after the country went to the polls.

The OECD was warning Ireland's housing boom was over while urging the Government to reign in its spending; Fine Gael leader Enda Kenny hailed the opposition party's 'phenomenal' performance in an election he would ultimately lose; on the other side of the Atlantic US President George W. Bush won approval from a divided congress for $100bn to keep fighting in Iraq.

Priscilla was too nervous to eat. She had spent the previous day in hospital with her dad and was worried about him, but even more so about the chain of events she had set in motion two weeks earlier.

At 7.20am she slipped out of the house, careful not to wake him, got into her car and released the handbrake.

She drove out of the estate, turned left down the Navan Road and a few hundred yards to the Maxol service station.

The private investigator and his sidekick were already there, sitting in the small white Ford van parked in the forecourt, like a couple of tradesmen on route to an early job.

Priscilla took in her surroundings but, as they agreed, she did not make direct eye contact or give any signals. She put petrol into the car and as she made her way out of the garage the white van followed a short distance behind.

She turned back into the estate and then indicated as she slowly approached the driveway of the house, signalling the address and the taxi parked outside to the men in the white van, who discreetly drove straight on.

By now Priscilla was a bundle of nerves. Her hands were clammy and her head fizzed with anxiety.

A few weeks earlier she had seen more texts from the same woman.

'Give me a call.'

'Babe, can you talk?'

But it still wasn't enough, there was too much plausible deniability, especially for an actor as talented as her husband.

She confided in a friend and got the number of the private investigator, who she met a fortnight ago at the Red Cow Hotel beside the M50.

She saw her chance after he announced a few weeks earlier that he'd be going away for the weekend to Cork with a mysterious new friend called Brian.

Priscilla was certain it was a lie. And if her suspicions were correct, she thought, she could finally nail him in the act.

But now, as she slid her key in the door, she was suddenly overcome by doubt and began to question her own sanity.

Her husband was just beginning to rise so she busied herself getting Ainie ready for school.

She helped her daughter into her navy-blue unform and put on her little light blue coloured tie.

Priscilla looked into the curious eyes of her nine-year-old child and suddenly felt wracked with guilt.

What in God's name am I doing to her father?

Maybe it's all in my head.

Am I just being paranoid?

But Priscilla knew she had to be sure; nothing could be left in doubt.

He came down the stairs, in unusually good form.

'I'll drop Ainie to school,' he told her.

No, Priscilla replied, I'll take her on my way to work, but he insisted.

She left the house at 7.50am and dialled the number as soon as she was out of view.

'I'm leaving now,' she told the man in the white van.

'He's leaving in 20 minutes, he's taking Ainie to school first.'

He dropped Ainie off at 8.20am and then returned to the house to collect his things.

Around the same time Priscilla's phone started to ring.

It was the hospital; Pat had taken a turn for the worse.

Priscilla froze. She had been dreading this moment for a long time. She immediately called her mother and then locked up the building.

Priscilla no longer cared about her sting operation. She jumped back in the car and tried calling her husband.

No answer.

She kept calling.

Again, and again and again.

No response.

Priscilla called her neighbour, who ran across to the house and knocked on the door until he answered.

'Priscilla is ringing trying to get you,' the neighbour told him.

'Will you give her a call – Pat's after taking a turn.'

But still he never called.

Priscilla collected Ann from the Navan Road.

There were no tears from her mother, just a quiet determination to get to her husband as quickly as she could.

But Priscilla was all over the place. She felt her hands tremble on the steering wheel. 'Mam, I'm not able to drive.'

Priscilla pulled over and called Cabra Garda Station, just a few yards away. The guard who answered knew Priscilla and Pat. He told her to come to the station, they'd have a car ready.

Priscilla felt as if she was having palpitations during the short drive to St James's Hospital on the other side of the Liffey.

They arrived at the hospital, thanked the guards for the lift and climbed the stairs as fast as they could.

The doctors were working on Pat by the time they reached the ward.

A short while later Priscilla and Ann were allowed in to see him.

Priscilla looked down at the pale, gaunt face of the gentle giant she adored. The sweat was rolling down his face.

'Hi dad,' she whispered.

'I'm not well love,' he said back softly. 'Not well.'

Pat's family began to arrive at the hospital.

Priscilla suddenly remembered Ainie. Who was going to collect her from school?

She tried calling her husband again, but still no answer.

In desperation, she called a friend who kindly agreed to pick up Ainie and look after her until Priscilla got home.

It was now just after 10am. The doctor came out and said he thought Pat had pneumonia. They were bringing him down to the intensive care unit.

Priscilla made up her mind. She called the PI and told him she was calling it off, her dad was dying in hospital.

But the sleuth urged her not to stand down the operation.

'This is the ideal time to catch him – you may not get another chance like this again,' he told her.

'Just let us keep going for another couple of hours.'

Priscilla had one question.

'Is he on the Cork Road or the Galway Road?'

'He's on the Galway Road.'

Priscilla felt her teeth clench.

'Right, keep going,' she said as she hung up and went back to her dying father.

In the ward, doctors were attaching drips to Pat as they prepared to move him to ICU.

Ann noticed her daughter in a distracted daze and asked where her husband was, but Priscilla didn't want to bother her mother with her marriage drama.

'He's gone to Cork, but he's on the way back,' she said, a wave of revulsion sweeping over her as she lied for him.

In desperation, she called a friend of his and asked him to get a message to her husband.

'Just tell him his father-in-law is dying.'

She went back to her father's bedside.

Pat held her hand and looked helplessly at his only child.

'I love you. I don't want to die. Where's Ainie?'

'I love you too dad,' she said back as she became aware of movement around her.

The senior nurse signalled to Priscilla and Ann.

There were no available ICU beds. They would have to transfer Pat to either St Vincent's on the other side of the city or to Galway University Hospital by helicopter.

Priscilla suddenly had an image of her husband hurtling down the motorway to Galway to some strange woman and felt a knot in her stomach.

It was as if Ann could read her mind.

'Gimme that phone,' she said, 'where's that bollix?'

Priscilla realised she couldn't cover for him anymore.

The stress of the day and all the years of pain and suffering came to a head in that moment.

She turned to her mother.

'Mam, he's no more in Cork than we are. He's in Galway. I have a PI on him mam ... he's been beating me up.'

Despite her grief, Ann felt a rush of anger as she hugged her daughter.

'I knew it,' she said. 'The bastard.'

She went back to Pat's bedside and found her husband's phone. He would always answer his father-in-law's calls, trying to keep on his good side.

Ann dialled his number. Finally – after ignoring dozens of calls from his wife – he picked up.

'Ann here,' she said curtly.

'I'm just letting you know Pat's dying. It's up to you what you want to do. We're waiting on an ICU bed. They have one in Galway or in Vincent's, but I'll let you know.'

'I'm on my way back,' he replied sullenly.

'Do what you want,' she said as she hung up.

He didn't mention Priscilla or ask how his wife was holding up. He also didn't ask about Ainie, who would be walking out of school in about an hour with no idea her beloved grandad was dying.

While they were waiting on news of the hospital transfer, Priscilla called the PI.

'He's just pulling into a housing estate in Galway, one of the roughest estates in the city,' he told her.

'We have photographs of him and her. He was eating a banana walking in the door in a pair of shorts and a t-shirt with his bag.'

Priscilla made a quick calculation; he would have known by then her father was dying, but still he continued on. He never turned the car around.

Just after 1pm, the senior nurse announced an ICU bed had become available in St Vincent's; they were transferring Pat by ambulance straight away.

Priscilla and Ann hurried to the hospital forecourt and hailed a taxi.

She felt a feeling of panic rise up from the pit of her stomach.

'Mam, how are we going to get through this?'

Ann's voice was firm.

'We'll get through it,' she promised Priscilla.

'We're going to be strong.

'We didn't see this coming – you didn't see this coming.

'None of us saw it, but we will get through it,' she said, squeezing her daughter's hand as the taxi swung into the hospital entrance.

Priscilla's phone pinged.

It was a text from her husband.

'How're you?'

If only you knew, Priscilla thought bitterly. She'd called him over 50 times and now – more than four hours later – this was all he could muster?

She tried to calm herself and then offered him some more rope.

'Where are you?'

'I'm in a church in Fermoy lighting a candle for your father,' he texted back.

Priscilla passed the phone to her mother.

'Mam, you're not going to believe this ...'

Ann read the text and looked up at Priscilla with venom in her eyes.

'I hope he burns in hell so I do.'

Just then, the ambulance arrived behind them.

Priscilla saw her father's foot sticking out the end of the trolley bed as they took him to intensive care and felt as if her heart would break.

A short time later the doctor arrived to give them an update.

Pat had been put into an induced coma.

'Look, there's no easy way to say this. It's touch and go but the next 24 hours are going to be crucial.'

Priscilla looked him straight in the eye.

'Are you saying he could die?'

'Yes.'

Priscilla sat beside Ann and held her hand. They occasionally tried to drink tea while they waited but never managed to finish a cup.

Shortly after 2pm the private investigator called back.

'He's gone to the school to collect the young fella with her.'

Priscilla's heart sank even further. This was a new low.

Here I am worrying about neighbours minding my daughter while my father is dying and he's collecting somebody else's child, she thought.

The PI's voice came back on the phone: 'Are you sure it's not his child, it's the image of him?'

'I don't know,' Priscilla exhaled, 'and I don't care anymore.'

Priscilla continued to get updates on her husband's movements while they waited for news of her dad.

The phone pinged again shortly after 5.30pm. He was finally on the road back to Dublin.

A short time later he stopped at a hotel on the outskirts of Galway. He disappeared for a few minutes before re-emerging dressed in a fresh pair of trousers and a shirt.

Priscilla would get the odd bland text from him as he edged closer to Dublin.

'Any news?'

Shortly before 8pm she got a final message from the PI saying the taxi was pulling into the hospital car park.

Priscilla signalled to her mother. 'He's on the way up.'

Ann looked around the room and leaned over to Priscilla.

'I'm making this decision – there is to be no confrontation in here, there is to be no hassle.

'If your dad passes or he doesn't pass, we are going to deal with this with respect.'

Moments later he arrived in the waiting room. Priscilla thought he looked red faced and under pressure, but he didn't even look at her.

He walked straight over to Ann.

'What's going on?'

Ann struggled to keep her cool.

'What's going on? If you had been here since this morning you'd know what was going on.'

Then she added: 'Did you collect your child?'

He didn't respond, then tried to change tack.

'Can I go in and see Pat?'

'No you can't,' Ann said as calmly as she could.

Just then, the doctor arrived and asked to speak to Priscilla and Ann on their own.

He was brief and to the point.

'Unfortunately I don't think Pat is going to see 12 o'clock tonight. So whatever you need to do and whoever you need to call, do it now.'

All the family gathered around Pat during his final moments.

Priscilla sat at one side of the bed holding her dad's hand. Ann sat opposite as Pat's breathing got shallower and shallower.

———

I was kissing him and hugging him and thanking him.

Everyone was talking to him, saying their goodbyes in their own way.

I leaned into his ear and told him: 'You're the only man who ever loved me unconditionally. We got incredible memories, but you can't fight this any longer.

'It was you who gave me everything.

'Let go, dad.'

Mam did the same.

He closed his eyes ... and then he was gone.

———

The nurse confirmed the time of death; 11.27pm. Priscilla felt her husband's hand on her shoulder and recoiled.

'Get away from me,' she hissed. 'Get the fuck away from me. No one will ever replace him.'

She felt as if she was hyperventilating.

'I want Ainie,' she cried out. 'I want Ainie – I want her!'

Priscilla tried to get up from the chair but straight away collapsed. She was only out for a few seconds. When she came through her husband was standing over her, trying to lift her off the ground.

'I'll never forgive you,' she said under her breath.

The doctor offered to give her something 'to calm you' but Priscilla didn't want to be numbed.

Ann temporarily buried her grief and took control.

She turned to the doctor and told him in no uncertain terms: 'There's to be no post-mortem carried out on my husband.'

She called the undertakers and made the initial arrangements.

Then she remembered Pat's false teeth; they had been taken out when he went on life support.

Priscilla asked her: 'What do you want his teeth for?'

'He's not getting bloody rigor mortis in his mouth – he'd die if he had no false teeth.'

Priscilla and Ann stayed up most the night going through everything that needed to be done.

Her husband was there too, but they didn't involve him in the conversation. He may as well have not been there.

After snatching a couple of hours' sleep, Priscilla collected Ainie from her neighbour's house first thing in the morning.

Despite her young age, Ainie was intuitive enough to know something was wrong.

'Mam, why didn't you collect me from school?'

Priscilla looked at her daughter and struggled to hold back the tears.

'Do you know the way I said Pat was sick for a long time Ainie?'

The little girl's eyes' widened. She instinctively knew what was coming.

'Holy God took granddad last night.'

Priscilla took Ainie in her arms as little screams of grief bellowed out of her.

'Why mam, why?'

She softly caressed the tears streaming down her daughter's face.

'You and I have to be strong now for granny because you and I are all she has now.'

Ainie nodded back at Priscilla as her chest heaved between sobs.

'Yes, we'll look after granny now.'

20

PRISCILLA WORKED through the complicated choreography of events in her head.

Her father would be buried the following Tuesday, May 29. Ainie's communion was on June 9. Once that was done and dusted she'd get her husband out of the house.

Pat Grainger was just 64 when he died. The morning of his funeral went by in a haze. Priscilla remembers the huge crowd, thousands of mourners who spilled out the back of the Church of Our Lady Help of Christians and onto the Navan Road.

Pat's old friend Paddy Cole played his favourite, Dublin in the Rare Old Times.

Priscilla, dressed in a black suit, white blouse and heels, addressed the mourners.

'We have lost our rock. My father was a rock to us, but also to a lot of people in this church.

'He was an amazing man, a bit of a Del Boy,' she smiled, drawing laughter from the congregation.

'Dad packed an awful lot into such a short life.

'He adored the ground mam walked on. Mam was his number one, I was his number two, but then Ainie became number two, and I became number three.

'We will live with all our wonderful memories.

'Goodbye dad, my rock. Sleep tight.'

Priscilla wiped the tears from her eyes as she stepped down from the altar to a standing ovation.

Pat was buried at Dardistown Cemetery.

His coffin was lowered into the ground to the accompaniment of Frank Sinatra's My Way, another of Pat's favourites.

Priscilla felt a hand on her shoulder.

'Get your hand off me,' she snapped as she shot a cold glance at her husband.

Afterwards, the funeral party retired to the Grand Hotel in Malahide, where Pat and Ann had held their wedding reception.

All the cousins from Leitrim were there. They all loved Pat. And they would kill her lying, cheating, abusive husband, Priscilla thought with a temporarily sense of satisfaction, if they knew what he was up to.

He was clearly uncomfortable, shifting nervously in his seat making pointless small talk.

Good, thought Priscilla, as she sipped her drink slowly. Let him stew.

Later, back at the house, he kept up the patter of small talk.

'Gorgeous funeral,' he kept saying.

Then he was on the phone again, texting somebody.

'I was just checking ...' he said after Priscilla clocked him.

'Yeah, well, I don't care,' she said softly.

'You don't know how hard it is. I've lost the only man that loved me.'

He stayed silent.

Priscilla put down her drink and went to bed.

The next morning she woke to the sound of her phone ringing.

It was Deirdre McLaughlin, Siobhan's mother.

'Priscilla, we're after getting word.

'Kearney is being charged for murder – he'll be in Dún Laoghaire court at 10 o'clock.'

Pat had always treated the McLaughlin children as if they were his own and they all loved him.

Now, they reckoned, he was already pulling a few strings for Siobhan from above.

Priscilla got out of bed and turned on the RTÉ news.

'The husband of Siobhan Kearney, who was found dead in her home in Goatstown, Dublin last year, has been charged with her murder.

'50-year-old Brian Kearney will appear in Dún Laoghaire District Court this morning ...'

All of Siobhan's family, her parents and seven siblings were there to see Brian Kearney being led into court.

They glanced occasionally at Kearney as he sat just yards away and remained emotionless throughout the short hearing. He chewed gum and avoided eye contact as details of his next court date were given.

Since Siobhan's murder her family had made several impassioned pleas for her killer to give themselves up. Before Christmas they held a candlelight vigil at the house in Goatstown where her body was found and spoke emotionally about their devastating loss.

'Siobhan was an adoring and adorable mother, sister and daughter,' her sister Aisling said at the time.

'Siobhan did not choose death, she always chose life. Someone else made the choice for her to choose death.'

Brian Kearney was given a life sentence in 2008 after he was found guilty by a majority verdict of 11 to 1 at the Central Criminal Court.

However, the grieving McLaughlin family would have to endure even more torture in late September 2022 when they received an email telling them Siobhan's killer will be eligible for a parole review in March 2023.

Deirdre McLaughlin says her family will never get over Siobhan's murder and that her killer should remain locked up for the rest of his life

———

He [Kearney] should be in prison for the rest of his days.

In America it's 30 years with no parole and that's the way it should be here.

They [Parole Review] ask me how I'm feeling? How dare they ask me how I feel.

I'm devastated, the whole family is devastated, every one of us.

Siobhan was just a spectacular daughter and I think of her every second of my life.

We all think of her every second of our lives. The children all grew up together, I had them all one after another, so they were all intertwined.

They're crazy about her still. Some of them still can't go down to the graveyard.

Her father looks after the grave, but they still can't [bring themselves to] go down there. That's how bad the pain is.

———

Siobhan's death also had a profound impact on Priscilla. When she learned her friend was murdered, she knew she had a potential life or death choice to make.
Unsurprisingly, Ainie's First Holy Communion was a rather sombre affair.

The previous week went by in a kind of blur for Priscilla.

The business, like many at the time, was now in deep trouble and Priscilla knew tough times lay ahead.

She met the PI in the Phoenix Park where he handed over the black and white evidence she needed.

On the day of the communion, Priscilla calmy went through the motions and tried as best she could to make it a special occasion for Ainie.

He was in a foul mood throughout.

Just you wait, thought Priscilla, as she struggled to keep her emotions intact.

Later, back at the house, she saw her chance.

He was upstairs lying on the bed watching the racing on television in a pair of boxer shorts with his hands behind his head.

Priscilla entered the room and stood at an angle where he couldn't see the photographs in her hand, partially tucked behind her back.

'Can I ask you a question?'

'Yeah, go on,' he replied without showing any real interest.

Priscilla took a deep breath.

'Do you know the day dad was dying ... where were you that day?'

He shot her a look of unease.

'In Fermoy ... I sent you a text.'

'I heard different,' she said, keeping his gaze. 'You were seen in Galway.'

His body language switched to defensive mode. His voice got louder.

'Yeah? Well, whoever saw me in Galway is fucking winding you up.'

He told her it was all in her head.

'You're going fucking doolally.'

Priscilla produced the photographs and flung them on the bed.

'Who's she?' she shouted at him.

'And who's he – the young fella?

'When you were collecting that young fella at 2pm from school I had to get strangers to collect our child.

'Now get the fuck out of here – I'll be back in half an hour and if you're not gone, I'll get you gone!'

Before he could say anything Priscilla was out the door and running down the stairs.

She was trembling and very afraid, but she felt in control.

Ainie was already safely strapped in the car. Priscilla went straight to her mother's house and poured herself a cup of tea.

When she returned an hour later she was relieved to find he was gone.

Priscilla called the local Garda station and told them she would be applying for a safety order in the morning.

She also called a locksmith and changed the locks on the front door.

But the next day he returned while Priscilla was out, climbed over the side wall and broke in through the back door and took the key.

Priscilla cursed herself for not changing the locks in the back, but she felt stronger now. She wouldn't let him terrorise her any longer.

She rang his number and he picked up straight away.

'I'm telling you,' she said in a low voice, 'if you come near this house again I'll get a barring order and I'll have you arrested and you won't be able to drive a taxi again.

'Don't come near me again.

'If you want to see your daughter, apply for access.'

Part 4

ESCAPE

21

June 14, 2007

FOR BERTIE Ahern, it would mark the pinnacle of a stellar political career. But as he rose to address the 30th Dáil for the first time he had no inkling of the dramatic downfall that lay just months ahead.

Despite the gathering economic storm clouds, the 'Teflon Taoiseach' had done it again, successfully seeing off the Fine Gael-Labour challenge from Enda Kenny and Pat Rabbitte.

Ahern was nominated by his consigliere Brian Cowen, the man who would replace him as Taoiseach less than a year later. The motion was seconded by the outgoing Green Party leader, Trevor Sargent.

Dressed in a dark blue suit, white shirt and stripped tie, the now three-time Taoiseach declared Ireland was living in a time of 'unprecedented peace and prosperity'.

But ominous economic headwinds were already blowing as the Taoiseach confidently outlined how wealth creation would be 'the engine' to drive improvements in social services and provide 'a sustainable future' for all.

Two months earlier, journalist Richard Curran's RTÉ documentary, 'Futureshock: Property Crash' warned of the economic collapse to come and questioned the role of banks and the construction sector in fuelling the Celtic Tiger bubble that would burst with devastating consequences.

And on the ground, many over-leveraged businesses were already beginning to feel the chill winds of recession.

22

PRISCILLA SLID her card into the ATM machine and whispered a prayer to Pat as she waited for the reassuring whirring sound of the cash filtering through the rollers.

The last month had felt like a lifetime. Her initial elation at getting her husband out of the house quickly evaporated as her new financial reality hit hard.

The catering business she built with her father was on the ropes. On the very day Pat was dying, a cheque for €35 bounced.

Priscilla felt as though her world was closing in on her. She was grieving for her dad while trying to be strong for Ainie and her mam. At the same time, she was fighting a losing battle to keep the business afloat.

There was little or no money coming in and Priscilla had no savings of her own to fall back on.

It had been difficult enough trying to keep herself and Ainie fed and clothed on the tiny allowance her husband allowed her to keep from her wages. But now even that small income had dried up and she didn't know how they would cope.

Priscilla took a deep breath and tried to ignore the knot forming in her belly.

She looked at the ATM screen.

Insufficient funds.

Well, that's it, she thought. We've got nothing.

Priscilla had endured tough times before, but never this level of poverty.

She was barely able to pay for petrol to take Ainie to school and back and, for the first time in her life, wasn't even able to tax her car.

Every now and then she would come across gardai on the road, some of whom she knew. She'd plead with them not to impound the vehicle and each time, much to her relief, they'd give her a pass with a warning to go straight home after she promised to get it sorted.

Over the next two years the three generations of Grainger women relied solely on Ann's pension and a credit union loan she took out in her name.

Aside from providing financial help to her daughter and granddaughter, Ann was the emotional glue that bound them together in the rollercoaster months after her husband's death.

But even the iron lady had a breaking point.

When it did come, Ann's grief hit her like a freight train, and she fell into a state of deep depression as she struggled to come to terms with the loss of the man who had been by her side for more than 40 years.

Priscilla knew it was her time to take the lead.

Despite having no money, she felt free for the first time in years. Priscilla grew in confidence as she juggled the twin roles of business owner and single mother, while trying to make sure her mam was ok.

With her husband and Pat gone, the three Grainger women soon fell into a new routine. Ann would take Ainie to school in the morning. Priscilla would collect her in the evening and a childminder would look after Ainie while she went back to work.

Despite his coldness towards her, Ainie missed her father.

Priscilla had sat down with her daughter and tried to explain some of the events that unfolded on the day her granddad died.

It was a hell of a lot for a nine-year-old child to absorb, but Priscilla felt it was better than lying to her daughter, who seemed to have an almost unnerving understanding of the complicated and at times terrifying world of the adults in her life.

A month after he left, Ainie told her mother she wanted to see her daddy.

She dreaded the thought of making contact with him, but despite everything she didn't want her only child not to have a relationship with her father.

Priscilla says he was initially reluctant to see Ainie, but they eventually agreed he could collect her every second Saturday from 12pm to 5pm.

Despite the family's dire financial situation, her husband did not provide any maintenance for six months. Priscilla dreaded the thought of Christmas approaching and not being able to afford a present for Ainie.

Although she hated herself for it, Priscilla eventually asked him for money to buy a bicycle for their daughter, but he refused.

'The taxi business is bad,' he told her with a straight face.

Priscilla looked around her bedroom and had an idea.

I sold anything I had of value ... my rings, my jewellery, my clothes.

I took some of his clothes and sold some of them as well at a car boot sale up in Glasnevin.

I put up ads and sold handbags and shoes.

He had physically and emotionally abused me; now this felt life another form of torture.

When we were together, he controlled all the finances, but this felt even worse.

He knew the business had hit rock bottom and my dad was dead.

Christmas was extremely tough, but we got through it somehow, with no help from him.

He just sat back, waiting for me to break.

Priscilla didn't realise it at the time, but despite being physically out of her life her husband was continuing to exert financial control over her.

At times she felt so lonely and desperate she even began to miss him.

She couldn't bear to think about the future, as a single mother and owner of a failing business.

Gradually, the doubts began to creep in.

'Maybe he's right – I am crazy and it's all my fault.

'I'm not cut out for business without my dad.

'I'll never amount to anything on my own.

'Am I being selfish?

'Did I make the right decision for Ainie?'

23

PRISCILLA WAS at rock bottom, financially and emotionally.

She just about managed to keep it together over Christmas. But as much as she tried to remain optimistic, she faced into the New Year full of dread.

She was simultaneously grieving the death of her father and her marriage, while trying to be strong for her mother and daughter.

The business she built with Pat was dying with him as recessionary storm clouds shuttered businesses across the country.

Soon the country itself would be insolvent, forcing a temporary loss of sovereignty as the International Monetary Fund (IMF) stepped in to take control of the nation's finances.

One Friday in late January, when she was at her lowest ebb, Priscilla's mobile pinged.

'I'm dropping up €500 to you,' he texted.

She wasn't ready to let her defences down just yet.

'Shove it up your arse,' she wrote back.

'When I asked you for money at Christmas to buy Ainie a bike you wouldn't. I had to sell the clothes off my back.'

But he kept chipping way.

The following day, when he arrived to collect Ainie, he tried to confront his wife at the door.

'I want to come in for a minute,' he told Priscilla.

'You're not coming in.'

'Just for a minute,' he pressed.

She stood firm.

'You can stand at the door but you're not getting in here.'

It was a miserable Irish January day, when the rain and biting cold could knock the syllables out of your sentences. Despite his wife's bullish demeanour, he sniffed a chink in the armour.

'Look,' he tried to reason with her, 'we need to sort this out.'

Priscilla could feel her resolve slipping.

'You've broken my heart; you've broken everything that belonged to me. Go away – I want nothing to do with you.'

She shut the door and burst into tears.

The calls and texts continued, sporadically at first.

With each contact he was sawing away at her defences, corroding her confidence.

Priscilla found herself questioning every decision she made. She despaired over whether she was doing the right thing for Ainie.

During one phone exchange in April, as Pat's first anniversary approached, she told her husband she wanted a divorce.

Given his pleas for reconciliation, Priscilla thought this would come as a hammer blow to him.

She expected shouting, abuse, threats … but instead he appeared calm.

'Since you've made up your mind I'll respect your decision,' he told her.

A few weeks earlier Priscilla would have been delighted to get this result, but as she put down the phone she began to worry.

Priscilla talked it over with her mother.

Straight away Ann smelled a rat.

'Be careful,' she warned her daughter, 'the finances on the houses aren't sorted and he knows it.'

Priscilla's heart sunk. After half a dozen re-mortgages their family home was more than €30,000 in arrears and in serious negative equity. Another €100,000 was owed on the Leitrim cottage and Priscilla was facing the threat of bankruptcy.

Furthermore, her name was on her parents' home, which she feared gave him a legal claim on the property.

She got advice from a solicitor friend of Pat's. He told her all the houses would have to be sold if she initiated separation proceedings.

Priscilla felt cornered. After all the hardship it took to finally get him out of the house, she now feared losing her home and that her mother could be left without a roof over her head.

Priscilla knew she had to box clever. But deep down she still held out some hope she could somehow save her marriage.

By early summer they were in regular contact. He insisted he was a changed man. He would get help for his gambling. But he stopped short of admitting he was an addict.

One morning he called up to the warehouse and asked Priscilla out to lunch.

I said yes.

It felt as though the wheels were turning in a direction and I needed to see where it would end up.

Financially, things were worse than ever, but part of me still believed there was hope, that he could change.

He said everything I wanted to hear.

He'd go to counselling for the gambling.

We'll be a family again, but it'll be different this time.

Ainie needs to have a father.

He said it was over with yer wan in Galway and promised there'd be no more affairs.

I knew the dangers. I knew there was a chance I could end up like Siobhan ... but at the time it felt like I didn't have much of a choice.

He moved back in early May, just days before the first anniversary of Pat's death and the day Priscilla's private investigation unravelled his secret affair and the elaborate web of lies he spun during her darkest hour.

Priscilla still clung to a hope that this time would be different. But the trust had been broken and she instinctively knew his promises could all be just a ploy, a temporary tactic to strengthen his position.

She certainly wasn't ready for intimacy and insisted he move into the back bedroom. She also ordered her husband to get tested 'to prove you're clean'.

He kept his promise to get help and attended two Gam-Anon meetings in June.

Gradually, Priscilla's defences relaxed. So much so that within a few weeks they agreed to go on a family holiday with Ann to Tenerife.

Ainie was thrilled and Priscilla allowed herself to believe they may have finally turned a corner.

The gentleman and charmer she fell for seemed to be back. She prayed the counselling had finally begun to tame the demons she wanted to blame for the gambling, the abuse and the violence.

Within two months of moving home he was back in the bedroom, but Priscilla was sleeping with one eye open.

24

HE WAS back where he needed to be. Back in control. And it wasn't long before he stopped going to counselling and the mood swings darkened the house again.

But this time it didn't come as a surprise to Priscilla. Despite her abiding hope they could somehow make the marriage work, she knew her reformed husband could be a conjuring act.

Deep down she expected it would come to this. She hoped for the best but, unbeknownst to her husband, Priscilla was planning for the worst.

The business wasn't making any money and any savings they had were long gone.

Priscilla knew something had to give. There was still a large mortgage on the Leitrim cottage so that ruled out a sale. After all the re-mortgages there wasn't much equity left on the family home, certainly not enough to leave enough change to buy somewhere new. His name was also on deeds of the house, and Priscilla knew he would be entitled to half the proceeds of any sale.

But Ann was now living alone in her spacious three-bedroom house on the Navan Road with more space than she needed.

Priscilla talked it over with her mother.

Ann agreed there was only one option open to Priscilla; sell the house and move in with her. They could use some of the leftover money to do up the house. It would slash their expenses and bring the three generations of Grainger women together under one roof where they could feel safe.

But there was one hitch; they'd need his consent. And Priscilla knew he would only go along with the plan if he believed that it was his idea.

She would have to choose her moment carefully.

Shortly afterwards, as more and more unpaid bills stacked up, she outlined the precariousness of their situation.

'We're going to end up with nothing – they'll take the house away and we'll be left on the street the way things are going,' she told him.

'We can't sell the cottage – there's more owed on it than what it's worth. The business is going down the tubes. What in God's name are we going to do?'

Suddenly, he had an idea. 'Why don't we sell our house? Your mother doesn't need all that space – we could build a granny flat for her and be able to take care of her.'

It suddenly dawned on Priscilla that her husband's lightbulb moment may have dawned sometime before this conversation. She would have to tread carefully. He was playing his own game.

Priscilla feigned reluctance.

'Ah, I don't know … she likes her own space … we'd be on top of each other … there'd have to be a lot of changes to the house … look, I'll ask her and see how she reacts …'

Ann was inscrutable.

'Oh, I don't know,' she said tiredly when they broached the subject with her together.

'I don't know, I'd have to think about it.'

The house was put on the market in December 2008, but by then the property crash was in full swing as home values plummeted.

Priscilla knew it was the worst possible time to sell, but they had no other choice.

Her husband's behaviour deteriorated further. He was back gambling and this time he wasn't even bothering to try and hide it.

He took out more Credit Union loans while Priscilla barely had enough to buy the basics.

The abuse was gradually getting worse. Occasionally the shouting would spill over into violence.

One night he kicked her on the shin and then threw the ironing board at her as she lay on the ground.

Thankfully, it didn't escalate but Priscilla found herself walking on eggshells for what felt like a lifetime while they tried to offload their house.

They would have to wait a full 12 months before they even had an offer. Eventually, in March 2010 it was sold for €286,000, leaving just €90,000 after the loan on their much-re-mortgaged home was cleared.

There were also further outstanding debts and expenses that made a serious dent in their remaining capital.

It was bittersweet moment for Priscilla as she left her marital home with so little, and after so many years of hardship.

I was glad to be out of it and going back to mam, to be honest.

Apart from Ainie I had nothing but bad memories of that place, but it was like we were starting all over again with nothing to show for it.

After the mortgage there was €90,000 left, but €40,000 of this had to pay off all the debts.

We'd also agreed to pay €40,000 towards the cost of building a flat for mam on the Navan Road property.

That left a grand total of €10,000, all in, and with no house after 15 miserable years of marriage.

But we were going to somewhere safer, we would be with mam.

We were a step closer to where we needed to be.

25

PRISCILLA AND Ainie soon settled into their new but familiar surroundings in the Navan Road with Ann.

Her husband became increasingly distant, staying out all night, ostensibly working, although Priscilla saw little evidence of it.

She secured the planning permission they needed to revamp the house to give Ann her own living quarters. In the meantime, Ainie moved into the box room upstairs while Priscilla and her husband took the backroom on the first floor.

Any intimacy they had when he first moved back had long since evaporated.

Priscilla felt they were more apart than ever. But she didn't mind so much anymore.

She had her mother and daughter beside her, like 'a safety net around me', and he wouldn't dare raise a hand to her in front of Ann.

Priscilla felt safer than she had done for years.

Finally, in March 2011, the builders moved in, and the house descended into a chaos of noise and destruction.

One Saturday, while her husband was at work, Priscilla and Ann came home to find the entire ceiling above the kitchen had caved in.

The contractor arrived at the scene shortly afterwards and gave his expert assessment.

'Fuck, this is bad.'

The house was a death trap.

Priscilla had enough. She called a local hotel and the family moved whatever clothes and possessions they needed to their temporary new home.

Ainie loved their new surroundings. It felt like they were on a long holiday and the staff doted on her, but Priscilla fretted about the cost.

Almost all the remaining €10,000 left over after the sale of the house was devoured by the mounting building costs.

Priscilla's wages and Ann's pension paid for the temporary accommodation costs. He didn't contribute a cent.

Priscilla hardly saw her husband during their stay at the hotel. She silently wished he'd ask her down to the bar for a drink or maybe bring her out for dinner once in a while, but he had no interest and stayed away for as long as he could, only returning to the room to sleep. She became convinced he was having another affair

———

Ainie got her holidays from school in June, but he was never around.

He was just going to work, coming back, sleeping, going to work ... and so on.

I knew he was at something, but I couldn't figure it out.

He never wanted to spend time with me and Ainie. Sometimes he'd bring Ainie swimming, but that was it.

To break the monotony, I'd bring her downstairs for something to eat or just sit there while she played with her colouring books.

I was very lonely, but I felt really bad for Ainie.
I knew she was craving some time and attention from her daddy, but he just didn't want to know.

———

Priscilla soon had another problem to contend with.

Towards the end of their hotel stay Ann became very sick. Priscilla brought her to a clinic nearby, but they couldn't find anything wrong.

Ann later underwent a scan at the Mater Hospital, which confirmed she had a serious infection in her hip.

She spent two months in hospital in considerable pain as she underwent a series of procedures. First, the infected hip was removed and replaced with a temporary one until the infection cleared. Then she had further surgery for a permanent replacement hip.

Finally back at the Navan Road, Priscilla found herself trying to look after her mother while taking care of Ainie and what was left of the business.

She hardly saw her husband, whose absences were now getting longer and more frequent. It was like living with a grumpy ghost who occasionally flittered in and out of their lives.

One night when her husband came home, Belle – their tiny four-year-old Teacup Yorkie – suddenly started snarling and barking at him. She's smelling someone else, Priscilla thought.

Although her husband was rarely home, he clearly liked the idea of being the man of the big house on the Navan Road.

Priscilla heard a few reports back from the Halfway House, just a couple of doors away, about him boasting, after a few pints, about living in a 'gaff worth €700,000'.

He constantly pestered Priscilla about getting his name on the deeds, forcing her to devise ever more creative explanations to put the conversation on the long finger.

'Over my dead body,' she said to herself, then felt the fear rising in her belly as she thought of Siobhan.

By now Priscilla just wanted him out, but she didn't have the ammunition she needed to pull the trigger.

One Saturday night in late October, the house phone rang.

Priscilla jumped. People rarely called her mam and dad's old landline and everyone in the house used their mobiles.

Priscilla picked up the handset.

A male Dublin accent she didn't recognise.

'Priscilla Grainger?'

'Yes,' she confirmed.

'You don't know me. You don't have a clue who I am. You'll never know me, but I'm just letting you know your husband is a pimp in Dublin 4.'

Priscilla went numb. It sounded crazy, but she couldn't contain the feeling of nausea creeping over her.

'What? You've got the wrong house. Sorry, my husband is a taxi driver.'

'Is his car the Black 04 Mercedes?' the voice said calmly.

Priscilla felt as if she was going to vomit.

'Yes,' she said. 'What ...'

'That's all I'm telling you. It's up to you to find out the rest.'

The line went dead.

26

PRISCILLA DIDN'T want to believe her husband was involved with prostitutes, but she also realised she had no idea what sort of double life he was leading when he walked out the door every evening.

He was hardly around anymore. And when he was, he always seemed to be on his phone, which he guarded more closely than ever.

He was often away for long periods, most of the time down the country 'on a job'.

Recently he'd been late turning up to collect Ainie from school.

Even the dog was sniffing and snarling at him.

It dawned on Priscilla she had no idea who the man now posing as her husband really was.

But she was determined to find out. And quickly.

He never left the mobile out of his sight. But despite the fact her business was now on a life support, Priscilla's company continued to pay his phone bill.

She couldn't act straight away. At the time Priscilla was nursing Ann, looking after Ainie, trying to keep the business afloat while preparing for another dreaded Christmas.

While juggling all these, she surreptitiously studied her husband closely on the rare occasions he was home. She noted his body language, the cockiness, the sneering attitude towards her. The way he'd always go outside to make or take a phone call.

Christmas passed, thankfully without any major blow ups.

One morning in early January Priscilla went back to the office and gathered up all his phone bills.

She grabbed a pen and paper made a note of every number she didn't recognise.

One stood out. Priscilla saw hundreds of calls listed to and from the mobile number she didn't recognise.

She googled the number.

In a flash, 'Sexy Suzie' appeared on her screen.

Priscilla was looking at a website for private escorts in Dublin.

'Holy sweet Jesus,' she whispered to herself as she scrolled down the screen and clicked some of the links.

'Sexy Suzie' was staring suggestively back at her, wearing only knickers and a bra. It was hard to make out the woman's facial features, but it was pretty obvious what she was selling.

Underneath her photograph there was a brief reference to Sexy Suzie's services and skillset and a contact number. It was the same as the one on her husband's phone bill.

Priscilla printed out the page and hid it under the floorboards in her office.

She felt sick to her stomach.

By now Priscilla knew the marriage was well and truly over. She had been waiting to find some evidence that would help her to get him out of their lives once and for all. She even guessed he was having an affair. But pimping out prostitutes?

Priscilla shuddered. She suddenly felt in a very unsafe place.

She decided not to say anything to Ann or, especially, to Ainie.

She needed to find out more.

The weeks passed and life went on as normal, at least for everyone else.

Priscilla tried to find more evidence. She went through his stuff while he was out, looking for papers, messages, numbers, a hidden mobile phone ... but nothing new materialised.

He came and went as he liked, seemingly without a care in the world, Priscilla noted bitterly.

Every now and then he'd play the good husband, calling Priscilla on his way home from work, whatever that was.

'Do you need anything at home?'

'No? Grand so.'

March marked the first anniversary since they moved into the Navan Road. He kept pestering Priscilla about getting his name on the deeds. She knew she was running out of excuses. And time.

Ainie's confirmation was coming up in May. After the nightmare they endured at the time of her communion, Priscilla was determined to make it a day out her daughter would remember for the right reasons.

The big day arrived and, much to Priscilla's relief, everything went off without a hitch.

The following weekend they organised a big post-confirmation party at the house. They had friends over. Ann organised karaoke. Priscilla took care of the catering herself.

The following Tuesday, while Ann was in Leitrim, he called Priscilla and suggested they go out for a drink.

It was the first time he had asked her out in ages. Priscilla agreed.

They were in Doheny & Nesbitt's on Baggot Street. Priscilla noticed he seemed to be under pressure.

Her husband had put on weight and was red faced. He was downing vodkas and Red Bull and kept going outside for a cigarette, leaving Priscilla sitting at the bar alone.

It was obvious he didn't want to be in her company. The feeling was more than mutual, but Priscilla was curious.

After a couple of joyless hours, they left the pub and were walking down Grafton Street on their way to Little Caesar's, one of their old restaurant haunts, to get something to eat.

Then the abuse started.

'I don't wanna go to fucking Little Caesar's! Eat a Burger King – it'll do ya.'

Priscilla didn't react. She knew what he was capable of when he was like this.

He went in and got a burger, but Priscila had lost her appetite.

As they walking to get a taxi, Priscilla tripped on something and stumbled.

He turned on her.

'What kind of fucking shoes have you on, ya stupid cunt ya?'

'Here we go,' thought Priscilla as she got to her feet and walked as calmly as she could towards the taxi rank.

She approached a cab and got in. He took one look at the driver and reared up again.

'I'm not fucking getting in with that fucking nigger,' he shouted, as people on the rank shifted nervously away from him.

He started to kick the side of the car.

Priscilla was mortified and beginning to feel very afraid.

'I'm really, really sorry,' she told the driver.

'Please bring me home … he's absolutely disgusting … whatever the damage is …'

'No, no,' the driver answered, shrugging his shoulders to let her know it was ok and he took her back to the Navan Road.

She put the key in the door and took a deep breath.

He was back within 10 minutes, like a raging bull in search of a China shop.

'You made a fucking show of me tonight,' he roared at her.

'You're the one who made a show of yourself, kicking that poor man's car. He did nothing to you,' she said back to him as she tried to make her way to the bedroom.

He was right behind Priscilla as she got to the door.

'You're a useless cunt,' he screamed at his wife before kicking her hard on the backside.

Priscilla collapsed through the door and fell onto the bed in agony.

Before he had a chance to follow through, Ainie was in the room, shouting at him to stop with tears in her eyes.

The 11-year-old girl pushed her father out the room, locked the door and threw her arms around Priscilla.

'Why did he do that mam?' she asked her mother as they could hear him swearing in the background.

But the storm, for now, had passed.

Priscilla turned to her daughter.

'This is going to stop – I promise you. I'm done.'

Although she failed to uncover more evidence of her husband's involvement in prostitution, Priscilla had another card up her sleeve.

Despite telling him she had withdrawn the complaint she made about him when she first got him out of their old house back in 2007, the court issued safety order was still in place.

Early the next morning she retrieved the paper from its hiding place and confronted him in the back bedroom.

She was trembling slightly, but her blood was still up from the night before.

'See this?' she said as she waved the order in front of him.

'Remember the day you told me to go in and get it withdrawn?

'Well, I never did. I want you out now – get the hell out of here.'

He looked shaken, and quite hungover. But he had no intention of going quietly.

'Go fuck off!' he shouted back. 'This is my house. Half of its mine. 'I'm staying right here!'

Priscilla read the signs. She grabbed Ainie by the hand and made for the door. She'd said her piece. Now it was time to get out of there while he was still undressed.

'You better be gone by the time I get back,' she called out as she closed the door behind them.

Priscilla took Ainie to a friend house's where she knew her daughter would be safe.

She called Ann down in Leitrim and told her mother about the prostitutes.

'What are you going to do?' she asked Priscilla.

'I'm getting him out – I have the safety order.'

Priscilla called a security firm she had heard of through a friend.

'Look, I haven't got any money right now, but I promise I'll pay you,' she told them.

'I need to get that man out of the house. He's capable of anything.'

Later that evening Priscilla drove back to the house. She muttered a prayer to Pat as she walked tentatively up to the front door.

She turned the key and breathed a sigh of relief. He was gone, but she knew he'd be back by 2am. He was like clockwork.

She called the security company again and within minutes two tall, muscular men were at her door.

Priscilla hadn't slept a wink and she was exhausted.

'Go to bed Priscilla,' one of the men told her. 'Try to get some sleep. We've got this.'

At 1.30am her husband returned to the house to find two strange vehicles and security men guarding the entrance.

'What's going on here – who are yous at my house?' he demanded.

'This is my house, I'm going in ...'

One of the security lads stepped forward, looked him in the eye and calmly said: 'No, you're not going in.'

He handed Priscilla's husband a copy of the order.

'There's a safety order against you. You gave her a beating last night.

'There's no reason for you to come back here. Now go!'

In the end, Priscilla noted with satisfaction, her hardman husband didn't even put up a fight.

In her eyes he suddenly became a very small man, driving off in the car she paid for with his tail between his legs.

Ann drove back from Leitrim the next morning.

The security guards left at 6am, but they promised Priscilla they'd keep an eye on the house and reassured her they were only a phone call away.

Priscilla was relieved to see her mother. She didn't think her husband would attack her in the house if Ann was there. The big brave bully was slightly afraid of the pint-sized pensioner, she thought, allowing herself a wry smile.

Priscilla called the local Garda station to report the breach of the safety order. She was put straight through to the desk sergeant.

She tried to remain calm as she relayed the events of the previous night as concisely as she could.

She told the sergeant about the safety order and what she knew of his double life.

'He's a taxi man involved with a hooker – you've got to help us.'

But her pleas fell on deaf ears.

The sergeant, to Priscilla's dismay, was refusing to take her complaint seriously.

She was 'a scorned wife', he told her. 'Go home, put your feet up and have a bottle of wine.'

Priscilla felt utterly deflated.

'Thanks for your compassion,' she said before hanging up.

Priscilla called the Carriage Office and told them her husband was using the taxi – her car – to drive prostitutes around the city. But they didn't take her seriously either.

'You've no evidence to prove it,' a civil servant said impassively.

Later that morning her husband arrived back at the house to get his stuff.

'I want my clothes, my records, my files,' he demanded.

Priscilla refused to let him in and called the local Garda station. Within a few minutes two officers were at the door.

Assured by the police presence, Priscilla agreed to let her husband into the house to retrieve his belongings.

He didn't know his wife had already taken photocopies of all his bank statements and the bookies' receipts he kept hidden in his wardrobe.

She'd also hidden some of his best clothes, including his good suit and jacket, which she would later sell when the money was tight.

Priscilla stayed calm, but as he was walking away, she couldn't resist a dig: 'You came in on a fucking bike and you're going out on a bike.'

But he still had her car.

27

SATURDAY, JUNE 18 seemed a fairly unremarkable summer day.

Outside Priscilla's front door on the Navan Road the world, as always, continued to turn.

Eight kilometres to the east, Robbie Williams and Take That were preparing to entertain a packed Croke Park. The Labour Party was about to nominate Michael D Higgins to contest the presidential election. And across the pond, at the Congressional County Club in Maryland, a 22-year-old Rory McIloy was on the verge of making history by becoming the youngest winner of the US Open since Bobby Jones in 1923.

None of these events, aside perhaps from a fleeting desire to see Robbie, registered with Priscilla.

After a hugely stressful two weeks she planned to take it easy. She badly needed to recharge her batteries.

Priscilla felt safer now he was gone, but the thought of him driving around the city in her car gnawed at her.

She had a spare key, which she found when she was going through his stuff. The security lads also told her they'd have no problem 'pulling him out of the car' if they could access the vehicle.

Priscilla was sitting up on her bed when her mobile rang.

It was a private number.

'Hello,' she answered, but the line went dead.

Almost immediately the phone rang again.

'Hello, can I speak to Priscilla?'

A woman's voice, high pitched with a Donegal accent.

'Speaking.'

The woman told Priscilla her name, before adding with a somewhat theatrical flourish, 'Aka Sexy Suzie ...'

She actually described herself as Sexy Suzie.

'I'm just letting you know,' she told Priscilla, 'I got what I wanted – your husband.'

'Well you're welcome to him,' Priscilla shot back, adding a few choice adjectives of her own as she tried to remain calm. 'Now,' she said, 'what is it you want?'

'We're going to destroy you.

'We'll have you out of the Navan Road.'

Jesus Christ, thought Priscilla, what fresh lunacy is this? Now she was being threatened by a prostitute in her own home.

Despite the revulsion she felt for the woman at the other end of the phone, Priscilla sensed an opportunity. She decided to change tack.

'Ok,' she told the woman who called herself Sexy Suzie. 'I don't know if you're a mother, but there's only one thing I need from my husband and then you're welcome to him.

'There are files, medical files, in the boot of the car and he won't drop them up to me. They're X-rays of Ainie's throat; she has thyroid difficulties and there's a problem with her blood.

'I need the files – it's my child's health for God's sake.'

Priscilla let the hook dangle mid-air.

There was silence for a few seconds as 'Suzie' chewed on it for a bit.

By the time she came back on the line her tone had changed.

'Ok … since you're putting it that way, I'll do that for you.'

She hung up as she went to consult with Priscilla's husband, her pimp, and called back after a few minutes.

'He won't drop them to you, so I'll tell you what I'll do. Come over to Charlotte Quay. If you pull in there, I'll get the files for you.'

In the space of a few minutes Sexy Suzie had lurched from threatening to 'destroy' Priscilla to conspiring with a concerned mother against her lover, who was also the father of this woman's child.

Priscilla was beginning to feel like a character in a Lewis Carroll fantasy, but she stuck to her new script. She needed this streetwalker on her side for now.

'That'd be great, thank you. She's in hospital tomorrow and the poor thing is in an awful way.

'As you can appreciate, she's going through terrible emotion and trauma with her dad not being at home …'

She left that one linger for a bit, then added: 'I won't be in a car, I'll be on the bus. I don't have a car, remember?'

The trap was set.

Priscilla's heart was racing, but the plan was clear in her head.

She called the two security lads and they agreed to help, even though it was Saturday.

'This is my chance to get my car back,' she told them. 'I have the key. I'll meet you at Charlotte Quay. I'm getting a taxi over there, you can follow behind.'

One of them asked her: 'Have you got that car in your name?'

Sure, she said, 'and I've just reported it's been stolen.'

The plan was for Priscilla to distract her husband while the two men took possession of her vehicle.

But as her taxi arrived at Charlotte Quay and she saw her car parked by the kerb – and Sexy Suzie standing there in all her glory and a long wig - something snapped in Priscilla.

She jumped out of the taxi and ran to the car. He was sitting in the driver seat with his arm leaning out the side window.

He never saw her coming. Priscilla opened the driver's door, grabbed his privates with her left hand and snatched the keys from the ignition with her right.

'Get the fuck out,' she screamed at him as his eyes widened in shock.

The two security lads were running as fast as they could down the hill, desperately trying to keep up with their client's improvised charge.

Priscilla was a human tempest; all the years of lies, coercive control and violence flared up and unleashed itself in a furious onslaught directed at her abuser.

———

I was like a madwoman, completely out of control.

I never knew strength like it. It was pure rage – at one moment I thought I was actually going to kill him.

His seatbelt was off and I grabbed him as hard as I could.

Out of the corner of my eye I could see the number 47 [bus] coming over the hill past Boland's Mills and, for a spilt second, I honestly thought I was going to drag him out of the car, [and throw him] straight under the bus.

Thankfully, I hesitated and by this stage the lads had caught up with me.

It took the two of them to pull me off.

I was still shouting at him – 'you dirty bastard ye' – as the security lads tried to get me away from him.

I grabbed the taxi sign off the roof and threw it on the ground.

Then I opened the boot. There were black sacks with his stuff still in them, so I threw them out too.

He was just standing there, gobsmacked.

'I told you – you came in on a fucking bike and you're going out on a bike!'

———

The security men finally managed to edge Priscilla into the back seat of her car. There was no way they were going to let her drive in that state.

One of them jumped into the driver's seat. The second man sat in beside Priscilla to try and keep her from jumping out.

Her husband didn't raise a finger to stop them. He just stood there at the side of the road, his mouth slightly agape. Frozen.

Sexy Suzie vertiginously tottered towards the car in her high heels.

'I'm sorry, I'm sorry ...' was all she could manage.

'Ah sorry me hole!' Priscilla shouted back as the driver turned the car and headed back in the direction of the city centre, leaving the prostitute and her pimp staring after them.

Priscilla's heart was pounding so fast she thought she'd explode.

There was hardly any traffic, and they were back on the Navan Road within 15 minutes.

Priscilla thanked her bodyguards again. But on this occasion they had only protected her from herself.

'I dunno what she brought us for,' one of them said to the other as they walked out the driveway.

28

PRISCILLA WAS worried about Ainie.

Her daughter always seemed mature beyond her years and, despite some of the horrific scenes she witnessed, Ainie generally seemed to a happy and fairly contented child.

She had lots of friends and was loved by her teachers and everyone who met her.

Ainie had grown up in an abusive environment, one in which there was little money for long periods of time, years sometimes, but she hardly ever complained.

Priscilla knew her father's absences and, when he was around, his indifference towards his daughter, had left a void in Ainie's life.

She was determined to fill the emotional gulf as best as she could, but sometimes even she had to admit defeat.

Ainie was 13 now, a teenager about to start secondary school. Priscilla noticed – as mothers do at that stage of their daughter's life – a big change had come over Ainie.

She became more withdrawn. At times it seemed as if she was in a world of her own.

'Mam, am I going to see dad this weekend?

'Why doesn't dad come to see me anymore? Was it because I was bold?'

Sometimes Priscilla struggled to respond. How do you explain to your daughter that her father doesn't want to see her?

She tried to be as honest as possible.

'Look, I might only be one mammy, but I'm mammy and daddy to you. We can't allow this man back into our lives and to hurt us anymore.'

Priscilla kept a lot back from her daughter. But even the sanitised version of the story was very difficult for a young girl to hear.

One morning, while Ainie was in her bedroom getting ready for school, Priscilla overheard her talking to herself.

'Maybe my dad will be over to collect me after school ...'

Priscilla sometimes felt as though her heart would break into a thousand pieces.

A transformation had come over Priscilla the day she got her car back. She no longer felt like a victim, or the worthless, unlovable creature he trained her to be. She felt strong and was determined to take control of her life. Her mother and daughter needed her more than ever and Priscilla vowed never to let a man, or anyone, make her feel that way again.

But after the initial feeling of euphoria, the reality of their circumstances set in.

Money, again, was a major issue. While Priscilla was still managing to keep the catering company above water, the three Grainger women often had to rely on Ann's pension to feed and clothe themselves.

Priscilla was broke and Ainie was about to start secondary school. She had to find money to pay for her uniform, her books, the fees.

Almost on cue, her husband began to make contact again.

The tone was different this time, Priscilla noted, more desperate.

'Please forgive me, I beg you ... give me another chance ... I'll do anything to make it right ... Ainie needs to have a father ...'

The gaslighting continued for weeks.

Priscilla was a lot stronger now and she instinctively guessed it was all just another smokescreen. The bullying and coercion wouldn't work anymore so now he was using the other weapons at his disposal; emotional and financial manipulation.

Despite his pleas to Priscilla, he had stopped paying maintenance, again leaving her to shoulder all the financial burden.

After repeatedly ignoring him, Priscilla eventually relented and agreed to meet him at Arnott's department store in the city centre. She hoped he'd at least have the decency to pay for his daughter's school uniform.

Priscilla was shocked by his appearance.

His whole face was bruised and marked. Her abuser had been given a right battering, Priscilla noted with a little satisfaction.

'What happened to you?'

'She beat me up,' he said, not able to look his wife in the eye.

He told her he had split up with the prostitute. He was living with a friend in Finglas. He begged her for one more chance.

Priscilla said no. But as she walked away she felt a storm of contrasting emotions brew inside her.

It was cold outside on the street and Priscilla shuddered as she felt the chill tingling at her spine. She pulled up the collar of her old coat for some warmth and hurried back to the car park before it started to pour.

Despite Priscilla's refusal to take him back, her husband sensed a weak spot.

Over the following weeks the texts became increasingly desperate, each one like a chisel tip tapping away at her defences.

One night, while Priscilla was sitting at home worrying about money, her phoned pinged.

'I can't cope without you or Ainie. Please help me.'

Priscilla sighed and reluctantly dialled his number.

'What do you want?' she demanded curtly, trying to keep the strength in her voice.

'I'm down in Dublin Port. I'm going to kill myself.'

'Christ,' she muttered through gritted teeth. Even now he still knew how to get under her skin.

She did her best to remain calm.

'You're only talking about killing yourself because you can't take responsibility for what you've done to your wife and child,' she told him.

'You destroyed our family; you destroyed our marriage. I'm not perfect – far from it – but I didn't go off with hookers and ...'

He didn't let her finish.

'I promise, I promise – I'll get help. I'll get help,' he pleaded with her.

'Then go off and get the help you need – you've been promising this for years.'

There was a slight pause, before his voice came back on the line. More subdued now.

'I've no money – she robbed me last night.'

Priscilla knew she should have slammed down the phone on him there and then, but something held her back.

Weakness? Curiosity? Epicaricacy?

She bit her lip as she found herself agreeing to meet him at the warehouse the next day.

He looked dreadful. His face was red and blotchy, his down-turned eyes appeared as if they were bulging from their sockets.

Priscilla thought he could be on drugs. She'd never thought him the type, but then she also didn't foresee her husband becoming a prostitute's pimp.

He wore a hunted expression. Again, Priscilla noticed he couldn't look her straight in the eye.

Part of her was enjoying the spectacle, seeing her abuser stand in front of her a broken man, begging for her forgiveness. But she'd learned the hard way not to let her defences down completely.

Her husband agreed to check himself into hospital to treat his gambling addiction, but he insisted he couldn't make the leap on his own.

To Priscilla this was a huge step. He'd lied time and time again about committing to counselling, but this – if it was genuine – was different.

Not to mention expensive. He couldn't afford to pay for the treatment so Priscilla's family health insurance, which she continued to pay, would have to cover it.

And now he was homeless.

Priscilla, against her better judgement, found herself agreeing to let him stay in the back bedroom for two nights before he was due to be admitted to the psychiatric hospital.

Ann was angry with Priscilla. She didn't want her son-in-law anywhere near her house after everything he had put them through.

'He's not well,' Priscilla tried to reason with her. 'He's Ainie's father. Dad wasn't well and we looked after him.'

'Well,' Ann replied, 'your father never abused or hit me.'

Temporarily back in the home, Ainie's father took her aside and made a vow: 'I promise you I'll be a better dad from now on. I'm going to the hospital tomorrow to get help.'

On Friday Priscilla drove her husband to the hospital where they were interviewed separately by senior medical staff.

She gave them all the gory details, leaving nothing out, but she wondered if he had been as open; his interrogation only seemed to last half the time.

Priscilla drove home alone trying to take it all in, struggling to balance feelings of self-loathing while still clinging onto some desperate hope that she could 'fix' her husband.

On Sunday he called her.

'They're letting me out for two hours if I want to see Ainie,' he told her.

Priscilla thought it was a bit early in the process for day release, but she let it go.

She was not, however, ready to allow her daughter to be on her own with him just yet.

'Ok, but Ainie will be with me – and that's if she wants to see you.'

Ainie was anxious to see her dad, so they picked him up from the hospital and took him to lunch.

After the meal he pulled up a chair close to the big screen TV and, to Priscilla's dismay, ordered himself a pint.

———

It was clear he had no interest in Ainie or me – he just wanted to be out of there [hospital].

United were playing on the television. That's all he wanted to do, he watched the game and ignored us.

I warned him he'd be tested when he got back to the hospital – they'd smell the drink on him a mile away.

The heavy work [treatment] was due to start the next day but he just shrugged his shoulders and turned back to the TV.

He was only out for two hours, and he couldn't even stay off the drink.

———

Priscilla dropped her husband back to the hospital and didn't hear from him for another two days.

On Tuesday he called her with a request. He needed some clean pyjamas and underwear, could she drop them down to him?

Priscilla was about to get up and drive to M&S, where she knew he liked to shop. She looked down at her own tattered threads and stopped herself.

She drove to Tesco in Finglas where she made straight for the bargain rail. She even found a pair of mismatched socks for 20 cents.

She was pretty sure now that her husband's mea culpa and promises to get better were just another ploy, borne of necessity.

But this time he overestimated his wife's susceptibility to his coercive control.

Even though she allowed him a temporary reprieve, Priscilla was under no illusion about what her husband was capable of. And at least, she thought, no one could ever accuse her of not giving him a chance.

When she arrived at the hospital the following morning he was in a foul mood.

He just grunted when she handed him the package.

'It's a fucking kip in here,' he said, looking balefully around the room.

But his wife was also in combative mood.

'Well, you're very lucky to be here. It's very expensive and I'm paying for your health insurance. Remember that?'

He went silent. Priscilla could see he was struggling to contain the fury bubbling up inside him.

She sat down and leaned over to him.

'Can I ask you a question?'

No response. She prodded further: 'What regrets have you got in your life?'

He stared up at her. Her husband's face was a picture of malice, his lip upturned in a sneer.

'Marrying you,' he hissed through clenched teeth.

There is it, thought Priscilla. The mask is off now.

'Well, now I know where I stand,' she said calmly.

Priscilla stood up with what grace she could muster, folded the towel she left for him at the end of the bed and walked out the door.

It was October 25, the day of Ann's 67th birthday. Priscilla had a few quid left over from buying his cheap underwear, so she stopped off on the way home and bought her mam some flowers.

'Thought you'd no money,' Ann said to her back at the house.

Ainie had made her granny a homemade card with a drawing of the three of them on the cover.

'I'll always find money for you two,' Priscilla said before turning to Ainie: 'Pet, will you go out of the kitchen for a bit? I need to talk to granny about something.'

But this time Ainie, who knew the conversation involved her father, and her by extension, wasn't for moving.

'I'm not leaving the kitchen,' she told her mother, 'I'm not leaving this room anymore. I see the two of ye going around hushing and whispering behind my back. I'm not stupid – I want to know what's going on.'

Priscilla looked at her daughter, the stubborn determination and tinge of sadness in her big blue eyes, then up at her mother, one of the strongest people she'd ever known. God how she loved them both.

Despite everything they'd been through, she felt lucky. He was the loser.

'Ok,' Priscilla said as she pulled up a chair, 'let's talk.'

29

THIS TIME Priscilla knew there could be no turning back.

Any slim hope she harboured of salvaging her marriage had, by now, well and truly evaporated.

Her entire focus now would be on Ainie and Ann. She knew she had to get him out of their lives once and for all, for all their sakes and sanity.

Her husband seemed to sense the change in his wife. To Priscilla, it seemed his loss of control over them was driving him to the brink of madness.

He bombarded his wife and child with calls and texts. But their silence only had the effect of intensifying the harassment.

In one text to Priscilla, he announced he was signing himself out of the hospital.

The following day, while Priscilla was at work, her phone rang. It was the consultant from the hospital, confirming what she already knew; he had checked out. It was the same consultant she had briefed about her husband's abusive behaviour on the day he was admitted.

Priscilla told him the marriage was over and that her husband was no longer her concern.

'Well Ms Grainger,' he told her. 'It's like this, you might be telling me that, but if what you told me is true [about abuse] your child could be put into care.'

Priscilla had the marks to remind her of her husband's propensity for violence, but the consultant's words still came as shock. It also strengthened her resolve.

A short time later Ann rang.

'This bollix is up here,' she said. 'He's after getting out of his car – now it won't start.'

Just then Priscilla saw his number flashing on the screen. 'Hold on mam, he's ringing here on the other line.'

'Hello, yes?' she said calmly.

'You better get me five fucking hundred euros now!' he shouted at her.

Priscilla stayed silent.

'Are you fucking listening to me?'

Priscilla took a deep breath. She wasn't going to take this from him any longer.

She summoned all of her strength.

'Go fuck yourself,' she spat back, trying to supress the twinge of fear in the pit of her stomach.

'Don't ring me again and don't ever go near my mother's door. I've told her to ring the guards ... you scumbag,' Priscilla threw in before hanging up.

I could feel myself shaking. I wasn't sure if it was fear, nerves, excitement ... maybe a bit of them all.

He was like a cornered rat and the mask was truly off, but I could feel the power he had over me was waning. He knew it too, of course, hence the threats.

Although the violence throughout our marriage wasn't a very regular thing; it always seemed to flare up when he felt he was losing control. That's when he was at his most dangerous and I knew this was where he was at now, standing outside the house in the lashing rain with nothing and a car that wouldn't start.

Anyway, he got the AA or whatever motor recovery crowd to come and restart the car ... and then he went off on his merry way.

He was gone!

That was on the Friday and the following Monday I heard he'd moved back in with Sexy Suzie. He had nothing at this point, so he had no choice whether he wanted to or not.

But I didn't care anymore. As far as I was concerned they were welcome to each other.

—————

No longer able to bully his wife into doing his bidding, her husband resorted to financial terrorism.

'I'll leave you fucking homeless,' he threatened in one text.

He refused to pay any maintenance and, with Christmas approaching, Priscilla was getting increasingly desperate.

She sold her own clothes, her shoes, her jewellery. Between that and Ann's pension – by now the business was on the verge of finally being wound down – they managed to keep their heads above water.

Priscilla was forced to borrow from friends just to get the basics in for Christmas, but it broke her heart that she had no money left over to get Ainie a present.

His new tactics were having the desired effect; on Christmas Eve Priscilla broke down and sent him a message, urging him to lodge some money so she could buy a present for their only child.

He was enjoying this now. 'Go fuck yourself,' he wrote back, paraphrasing the last words Priscilla had spoken to him. 'Remember the day you wouldn't even give me €500?'

He didn't contact his daughter over Christmas.

Despite their circumstances, the three Grainger women rallied whatever resources they could muster and managed to get through the day. They had each other and that's all that mattered now.

By now, Priscilla admits, she was in a state of 'all-out war' with her husband.

Finally free of him, her new year resolution for 2012 was to somehow put her family on a more secure financial footing.

Her hatred, she recalls, gave her strength. And she would need every ounce of it to weather the coming storm.

Their finances were in a perilous state. The mortgage on the Navan Road was €3,000 in arrears. The cottage in Leitrim was €123,000 behind in payments. He was refusing to pay maintenance and didn't contribute a cent towards their shared debt mountain.

Ainie returned to school on January 12. It was a bitterly cold day and after school Priscilla took her daughter for a hot chocolate to put some warmth into their bones.

On the drive home, Priscilla's phone rang. It was her husband.

'I want to talk to Ainie,' he said gruffly.

'Well I don't know if Ainie wants to talk to you – we haven't heard from you since before Christmas ...'

Before she could say anything more he exploded: 'I'm fucking telling you – you better put me onto fucking Ainie or I'll fucking kill you.'

Priscilla let the threat hang in air.

'I have you now,' she said to herself before hanging up.

Priscilla immediately called the Garda Station.

She told them of the threat against her life, the years of abuse she had suffered at the hands of her husband and the outstanding safety order.

'I'm telling you straight he is going to murder me unless something is done,' she told the Garda.

This time her plea was taken more seriously. A few days later Priscilla's husband was formally arrested and charged at Blanchardstown Garda Station with threatening to kill his wife.

Priscilla was also determined to expose her husband's criminal enterprise.

She called the private investigator who helped to expose his affair in Galway and told him everything she knew about his links to prostitution.

Over the coming weeks the PI compiled a damning dossier of her husband's sex-for-sale racket.

He was able to confirm Priscilla's husband and Sexy Suzie were operating out of an apartment in one of the city's most upmarket addresses in the heart of Dublin 4. Priscilla learned they paid €1,500 rent a month for the apartment, despite insisting he couldn't afford to pay any maintenance.

The investigator was quickly able to establish her husband and Sexy Suzie's modus operandi. He would meet customers outside the apartment, take the money and then drive a short distance down the road. Then he would park up, sometimes for up to an hour, talking on one of his two mobile phones before driving back to the apartment to meet the next client.

Priscilla had the evidence she needed; now she just needed the story to get out.

She got in contact with Mick McCaffrey, an award-winning crime reporter with the Sunday World.

Priscilla gave Mick the evidence her PI had gathered and the reporter agreed to meet her in court when her husband was due to be charged.

That morning Priscilla dropped Ainie to school as usual before she and Ann headed into the court.

Sexy Suzie was there, Priscilla noted, dressed for the occasion in a skimpy leather skirt and lace tights.

Priscilla's husband pleaded guilty to breaching the safety order and was given a 12-month suspended sentence. He was also ordered to donate €150 to Women's Aid, but he avoided a criminal conviction and the loss of his taxi licence.

Despite only getting a rap on the knuckles, he was furious at being hauled to court.

Passing Priscilla outside the court, he told her – in front of witnesses – 'I'll take the fucking house on you Grainger.'

Mick and the Sunday World team swung into action. Over the next 10 days they tracked Sexy Suzie and her pimp as he ferried his girlfriend across the city to meet various clients.

Mick also discovered the prostitute – despite advertising a slew of acrobatic sexual services – was suing a driver and his insurance company for €100,000 for serious injuries she claimed she sustained in a car crash.

After gathering the evidence he needed, Mick, posing as a client, called Suzie's number and arranged an appointment.

When he arrived at the apartment he observed Priscilla's husband sitting in his taxi outside. He went inside and spoke briefly to the prostitute before the undercover reporter, in the parlance of the classic tabloid sting, made his excuses and left.

The Sunday World carried their exposé on the front page.

'SEXY SUESY', screamed the headline, with the strapline: 'Woman suing in €100k 'bad back' court case is €2,000-a-day "Sexy Suzie".'

Inside, the article was spread over two pages, exposing the 'cheeky hooker' and the 'athletic sexual services' she was providing despite claiming in her High Court action that she was unable to flex her arms or back.

It also detailed her pimp's involvement in the operation, saying the newspaper 'tracked her down to an apartment block in leafy Dublin 4 where she lives with her brute partner … who has just been convicted of making threats to kill his estranged wife.'

The report went on to say how the hooker 'advertises herself on vice websites as a 28-year-old professional escort who charges €200 an hour for seedy sex romps'.

But, the article revealed, the prostitute 'is in fact 38 years old and tries to pass herself off as a respectable antique dealer'.

It detailed how the newspaper's undercover team observed Sexy Suzie 'travelling to hotels and private houses across Dublin' to meet clients.

The report also noted how she 'has been stopped on several occasions plying her trade on the streets,' adding she admitted telling gardai she had a 'cocaine habit.'

The report noted how Suzie's web page provides 'a menu of services,' but it warned: 'Most of it is too graphic for a family newspaper.

'Her web page describes Suzie as being aged 28 and boasts that she "delivers a fantastic service and is a popular young Irish lady. She enjoys having fun and is eager to please. Also enjoys meeting couples."'

The article added: 'If punters want Suzie to accompany them to functions, they can pay her €500 for a three-hour dinner date, €1,200 for her to stay with them all night and €2,000 for an enjoyable "girlfriend experience".

Describing the hours leading up to the reporter's encounter with the escort, the article stated: 'We observed her attending the Mater Private Hospital in Dublin last Thursday where it is believed she had physiotherapy.'

But it colourfully added: 'The session must have worked wonders because within an hour she was inviting the Sunday World to her €1,500-a-month rented apartment for an energetic sex session.

'Sexy Suzy buzzed our undercover reporter into the apartment building. After introducing herself in a soft Donegal accent, she asked if half an hour was ok and said it would set us back €100.

'She led our man into a dingy bedroom with an old double bed and an antique light that was supposed to add to the "romantic ambience".

'She asked us to leave €100 on the bedside locker and to relax and that she would need to give our reporter a shower before getting down to business.

'We then said we had changed our mind. She appeared offended by our U-turn and asked: "Have I done something wrong?"'

The newspaper then went on to detail the prostitute and pimp's responses when they were confronted by the Sunday World team.

Despite being exposed as a prostitute, Sexy Suzie continued to insist she suffered serious injuries in a head-on collision and that she was entitled to compensation.

Priscilla's husband claimed that, although 'Sexy Suzie' was his girlfriend, he was 'not responsible' for what she did for a living.

Despite this, the newspaper was able to detail how it tracked him driving 'Suzie' to her 'various appointments across the city'.

It also reported details of his recent court appearance.

'He appeared before Dublin District Court where he pleaded guilty to making a threat to kill his estranged wife last year.'

It also noted his wife had a safety order against him since 2007 'following frequent complaints to gardai about domestic violence'.

For Priscilla, her husband's conviction and exposure in the media was a significant turning point.

It saved us. With all of the prostitution stuff out in the open and his suspended sentence it meant that, for the first time in a very long time, we felt safe.

I felt myself getting stronger and stronger; I was still afraid of him, but I knew I was never going to let that man bully or control me ever again.

The table had turned full circle; now he was the hunted one. I knew now that I was cleverer than him and the [media] coverage gave me great confidence. But he was humiliated and much diminished after that.

I kept going to counselling and although we were still struggling financially, I was able to start looking to the future with hope, without the feeling of fear and dread that was there before.

It felt as if we finally had some peace.

30

PRISCILLA'S 'PEACE' only lasted a fortnight.

In the early hours of March 24 she was abruptly woken by a phone call. Sexy Suzie was at the end of the line.

The enraged prostitute proceeded to subject Priscilla to a sickening volley of abuse – even accusing her and Ann of child abuse – before telling her: 'I'm on the way up now – we're going to fucking kill you.'

Priscilla hung up and rang the local Garda station.

Ainie heard the commotion and came down the stairs in her pyjamas, clutching her little dog Belle.

Priscilla threw an overcoat over her daughter, bundled her and Belle into the car and drove the short distance to the station.

'Please, please – you have to help us,' she told the duty desk sergeant. This time she had all the proof she needed. And while she was making her complaint to the Garda her phone continued to ring; she received a total of 12 missed calls along with several voice messages from 'Suzie' while she was at the station.

Ann Grainger also received six missed calls and abusive voice messages from the prostitute the following day.

Confronted with the damning evidence, 'Suzie' agreed to present herself to gardai and admitted making the calls.

Despite the horrific threats, Priscilla refused to be intimidated and was determined to press charges.

And when the case eventually came before Dublin District Court at the end of 2013 and early 2014, the media were there to cover it.

The Evening Herald reported how the defendant pleaded guilty to two counts of sending telephone messages of 'a grossly offensive, indecent, obscene or menacing nature at an address at Navan Road, Dublin'.

The court heard how she 'accused her partner's estranged wife of being a child abuser in a series of obscene, menacing voicemails', adding she had 'flipped' over a previous newspaper article that had been written about her.

At the time, the court heard, the defendant 'was upset about serious allegations contained in the report in a Sunday paper which her defence maintained was defamatory and an invasion of her privacy'.

Undeterred, the Sunday World also published a follow-up article. Headlined, SEXY SUZIE'S 'A DIRTY CALL GIRL', the report added: 'Prostitute who tried to claim €100k compo for car crash while doing tricks for clients charged over vile voicemails.'

The article went on to say Sexy Suzie was 'charged under the Telecommunications Act with leaving obscene messages on the mobile phones of two named individuals'.

She was given a 12-month suspended sentence and ordered to donate €250 to Women's Aid.

Priscilla, Ainie and Ann Grainger never heard from 'Sexy Suzie' ever again.

With her abuser and his girlfriend out of the way, Priscilla found herself having to face down a new foe that was threatening her family's security. The bank.

The catering company had finally gone under, leaving Priscilla and Ainie again having to rely on Ann's pension.

They were struggling to keep up the repayments on the Navan Road, while Cully Cottage sank deeper into arrears.

Despite their best efforts, in February 2016 the bank threatened to repossess the cottage.

Priscilla was furious. Her husband's name was also on the deeds, but the bank was only coming after her for the arrears.

After initially refusing to meet her, officials eventually agreed to a sit-down summit when Priscilla told them she had information that was potentially extremely damaging for the bank.

In February 2016 Priscilla and Ann met with executives at the bank's headquarters, which was located just a stone's throw from the street where her husband and his girlfriend were still operating their brothel.

Priscilla produced photographs, taken by her private investigator, of what appeared to be bank officials entering the apartment at lunch time, emerging between 30 minutes and an hour later before returning to their place of work.

She pointed out the apartment and her husband's rented car parked outside.

Priscilla threatened to go public with the evidence.

It worked, but we shouldn't have had to go to these types of lengths to make them sit up and treat us with a bit of respect.

I was the only one making all the running with the repayments, but they always came after me, the woman. He got away scot free without having to pay any of the arrears back.

Eventually, they relented and told us just to pay what we could, which we were doing already.

I asked them to put it in writing, but they refused; the deal was that nothing would be written down, but at least it put a stop to the threatening letters.

The total amount owed was €130,000 and, thank God, that's all paid off now.

Gradually, the Graingers' financial position improved. Priscilla had always been a natural entrepreneur and once she got over the disappointment of losing the company she decided – just like the family did almost 30 years before – to transform their home into a hospitality business.

Priscilla and Ainie went to work, emptying the rooms of furniture to make way for more beds to rent out to students.

They crammed their own beds into the sitting room along with a fridge. The room would be their living space for 18 months, a tiny bedsit within the house which was now filled with paying tenants.

When she heard Dublin City Council was looking for B&Bs to take on emergency accommodation, Priscilla tweaked her business model. She rented four rooms to the local authority, boosting her income and giving the family a financial security they had not known for years.

A close friend of Priscilla's gave her a loan of €10,000 to build a cabin in the back garden.

Priscilla and Ainie moved into the modest two-bedroom structure to free up more rental space in the house.

But after spending a year and a half living in their cramped sitting room, 'it was like moving into Buckingham Palace,' Priscilla recalls.

'We had our own bedroom, we had a little ensuite, we had a sitting room and a television – it was heaven!'

31

THE B&B business grew in tandem with Priscilla's renewed confidence.

Although prone to occasional bouts of sadness and anxiety she was feeling stronger every week.

But Ainie, she noticed, had become more withdrawn.

It saddened Priscilla that her daughter had been exposed to things a girl her age should never have to endure.

Ainie went from being a happy and relatively carefree child with lots of friends who loved school to an anxious teenager who was becoming increasingly dependent on her mother. She went everywhere with Priscilla and became anxious when her mother was not around.

Ainie remembers a big change coming over her after her father had gone, which coincided with her finishing primary school.

It was a couple of days before the summer holidays.

I was a bit all over the place, trying to understand what was going on. I mean, at 13, you don't know what you're supposed to be doing; you're growing up and you're making different friends. It's all different.

It's a tough time and it's when you're at your maddest as well, but it's also a time when things that happen to you, when you're younger, you start playing them out.

Everything has an impact on you. If you're sad about something and you don't know why, you end up punching a wall, or you end up going on the mitch [from school] or whatever it is.

After my dad was gone, I became like a prisoner in my room. I did love school [up until then], but I just refused point blank; I did not want to go to school.

I only wanted to be with my mam. I clung to her a lot when I was a teenager. Friends would be asking me to do things and I'd be like, 'no, I'm staying at home with my mam.'

I clung to her a lot more when I was 13, 14, because I think the two of us didn't really know what to be doing. He [father] wasn't here.

When problems came up in school my mam obviously had to explain: 'Her dad's just left, give her a bit of time …'

It wasn't like I was getting into trouble for acting out, I just became the quietest girl in school. The teachers wouldn't even know I was there. I became invisible. I used to just sit there … I wouldn't have a clue what was going on.'

It was difficult enough trying to cope with the loss of her father. But seeing his name splashed across a national newspaper with his prostitute girlfriend was devastating for the 13-year-old.

Ainie remembers Priscilla tentatively telling her a few days before the article was published that he was going to be in the paper, but she didn't really understand why.

Priscilla was torn over whether or not to tell her daughter about the article. She discussed it with Ann.

'Look, either way she's going to find out – whether it's someone in school or whoever,' her mother pointed out.

Priscilla decided being up front was the lesser of two evils.

The night before the article came out Priscilla arranged for a security man to stay in the house as a precautionary measure.

Perhaps reflecting the chaos of their lives at the time, Ainie recalls not feeling anything particularly unusual about a strange man staying in her house.

'He was a really nice man, I don't remember his name, but I remember him saying, "Ainie, I'm just here so you can get some sleep tonight. Everything's going to be fine."

'That's all he kept saying to me. I remember mam telling me there's a man sitting downstairs "just in case". And I was fine with that, I felt totally protected.

'It didn't feel weird. I trusted my mam, you know, that everything was going to be okay.'

But her sense of security was shattered as soon as she saw the article.

———

I'll never forget it; it felt like a death in the family.

Mam tried to be delicate about it, but you can imagine what it was like for a 13-year-old girl to see her father with a prostitute in a newspaper.

She brought the paper and asked if I wanted to see it.

I said yeah. I opened the paper and I immediately burst into tears.

I remember reading 'couple sessions available' and I thought, 'How can my dad be involved in that?'

I struggled to put it all together in my head.

I was like, 'Who is this man? Is he really my dad?'

That's all I kept thinking, 'Is he my dad?'

On the Monday, I didn't go to school, but I went in on the Tuesday.

We were coming out of the library and the head teacher pulled me aside and said: 'Ainie, your mam rang me about the article, but it's okay. We're here for you.'

It was in the middle of the hall with all the other kids walking around.

I just went, 'Aw yeah, thanks very much.'

She meant well, but it made me feel even more like I didn't want to be there.

———————

Ainie also had to endure the abusive late night phone calls from 'Sexy Suzie'; the threats, the foul language, being bundled into the car and brought to the Garda station for her safety.

Ann was disgusted at her son-in-law's behaviour, and the impact it had on Ainie. But she was still careful not to badmouth Ainie's father in front of her granddaughter. And when Priscilla brought her husband up, sometimes after a few drinks, Ann was quick to shut down the conversation.

'Don't Priscilla,' she'd tell her daughter. 'I know it hurts, but he's still her father. Let her make up her own mind.'

Priscilla and Ann did their best to protect Ainie from the fallout of her parents' marriage and her father's activities.

They included her in almost all their discussions and did everything they could to fill the emotional void left by her father.

But they knew couldn't do it alone.

Priscilla organised counselling for Ainie, which Ann says was hugely important in helping the teenager to cope with her trauma.

———

Ainie went through a very tough time; she saw and experienced things girls of her age shouldn't have to.

Priscilla, of course, was going through it all as well at the same time and she needed help too, but we came together and supported each other through it as best we could.

Ainie had to grow up very fast but thank God she got the counselling and got through it.

She didn't like or agree with all of them [counsellors] but I said to her: 'If you don't feel comfortable, don't go.'

And I'd say it to Priscilla, 'She needs to be comfortable; she needs to be able to open up the way she should be able to – otherwise it's a waste of your money.'

———

With the benefit of regular counselling and the support of her mother and grandmother, Ainie gradually grew in confidence.

Although she tried her best not to allow him to leave a void in her life, she was determined to tell her father a few home truths of her own.

In December 2017 she finally confronted her dad, who she hadn't seen for five years.

Ainie didn't want to have a stand-up argument with her father or give him an excuse to just walk away again. Instead, she decided to put her feelings down on paper in the hope it would have more impact.

Now a young woman of 19, Ainie told him he was 'a disgrace' as a father and husband.

As far as she was concerned, their DNA was the only thing they had in common.

He would never get to walk her down the aisle or meet his grandchildren.

She ended the letter saying she would never forgive him for the way he treated his wife and daughter.

Weeks, months and years passed, but he never responded to his daughter's letter.

Ainie never heard from her father again.

Part 5

AFTERMATH

32

January 27, 2020

AINIE GRAINGER breathed out slowly as she took to the podium to address Cambridge Union, the oldest debating society in the world.

The 21-year-old Dublin woman, who freely admits she had 'no interest in school', now found herself on the stage that had hosted world leaders including Theodore Roosevelt, Ronald Reagan, Winston Churchill, Margaret Thatcher, the Dalai Lama and luminaries such as Bill Gates and Stephen Hawking, to name a few.

Ainie was invited to address the union as part of a special debate on domestic abuse alongside Lyndsey Dearlove, the head of the UK SAYS NO MORE group and Elizabeth Woodcraft, the author and former barrister who helped advise on the British 1976 Matrimonial and Domestic Abuse Bill.

She was nervous, but also the right side of angry. After years of campaigning alongside her mother, she had grown sick of politicians' empty promises to tackle the spectre of domestic violence.

During her speech, Ainie accused successive governments of merely paying 'lip service' to the issue without taking any real action.

With a general election looming, she urged the incoming administration to sit up and finally listen to the voices of survivors and child victims of domestic abuse.

She told the audience: 'They know that something needs to be done, but again it is just brushed under the carpet.'

Ainie's address, just weeks before the first wave of Covid-19 swept over Europe and Ireland, added: 'I don't know what is coming down the line, I'm scared for young people in Ireland because the problem is getting worse, but nothing is being done.'

Recalling some of her personal experiences, she told those gathered: 'At the time I didn't understand [why the abuse was happening], I just thought I was being punished because I was bold.

'The screaming, the shouting ... listening to it on a Friday and Saturday night when you should be watching a film, playing with your toys – that didn't happen for me.

'I remember one night, I was in bed, it was late and I was looking at the wall listening to the screaming.

'I was just praying: please God, how long will I have to put up with this?'

Talking about the moment her mother finally plucked up the courage to get them out, she told the audience: 'It wasn't easy for her to leave – it's never easy to leave. It's never easy to just walk out that door.'

Ainie also used the platform to urge young people to destigmatise domestic violence by talking openly about their experiences.

'Domestic abuse in Ireland remains a stigma, something that is brushed under the carpet that nobody wants to talk about.

'Please, I would urge anyone who is experiencing domestic violence to talk to somebody, anybody that they can.

'And to them [victims] I would say: please do not be afraid, because I promise you – there is light at the end of the tunnel,' she said to applause.

It had been a busy few years for Ainie and her mother. After struggling through secondary school, the young woman instinctively knew she wanted to help other victims of domestic abuse, but first she needed to find her own voice.

The seeds for her future advocacy work were sown during a trip to New York with Priscilla in November 2013. They were travelling to the city for her cousin Tara's graduation as an officer of the New York Police Department [NYPD].

While stateside, Priscilla was anxious to learn more about domestic violence initiatives in the US and how the authorities there were tackling the problem.

They met with Kathleen O'Reilly, the Commanding Officer of the NYPD Domestic Violence Unit, who gave Priscilla and Ainie a detailed insight into how domestic abuse cases are policed in the city.

One key difference between the approach there and in Ireland, Priscilla noted, was that domestic abuse victims did not have to make a statement to officers who called to the scene. The New York cops generally had far greater leeway when it came to identifying and responding to the immediate needs of victims in potential domestic abuse cases.

Priscilla and Ainie also met with Brian Martin, the founder of the New York based charity CDV.org, or the Childhood Domestic Violence Association.

Ainie's two-hour conversation with Mr Martin at the CDV.org headquarters on Madison Avenue would leave an indelible mark on the teenager.

———

I was honoured to meet Brian. He's from New York and was a child of domestic violence and had written a book about his experience.

He sat down and spoke to me and even though I had never met this person, it instinctively felt like he was talking my language.

He was able to help me to understand what I was going through from a child's experience of domestic abuse, and I was able to talk and make sense of how I was feeling.

At the end of the meeting Brian said they'd love me to become an advocate for CDV.org. I was delighted, although to be honest I didn't even fully know what an advocate was at the time!

After the meeting my cousin Tara organised a visit to a women's shelter, a refuge, in a very tough part of Brooklyn.

I'll never forget it ... a big building full of women and children and shelves full of books and toys.

There were lots of children my age there. I remember thinking: 'We've had it bad, but then you look at what these kids went through, they literally have nothing ...'

———

The New York trip was a major milestone in Ainie and Priscilla's transformation from victims to advocates, a metamorphosis from survivor to saviour as they plotted a new course to help other victims of domestic violence.

Priscilla was determined to do something to help other victims. She was angry at the system, which she felt let her and Ainie down badly in their hour of need.

The refuges were almost always full up and Priscilla felt there wasn't any frontline organisation out there to provide the type of immediate and practical help domestic violence survivors need to take the first crucial steps to escape their abuser.

After their New York visit, Priscilla and Ainie spent days discussing how they could help other women and men who found themselves in similar desperate situations. How to access legal services, apply for financial aid, counselling, food, nappies, a toothbrush … sometimes the smallest things can be the difference between a victim taking the decision to escape and staying with their abuser.

Priscilla understood from bitter experience just how difficult it was to take those first steps to freedom. It had taken her years and several attempts before she could finally break free. But if the proper supports were in place, maybe others wouldn't find it so difficult.

Priscilla and Ainie discussed the idea of establishing a new frontline support group in Ireland with a leading family law solicitor who agreed to provide whatever legal advice or direction they needed to help victims. Stop Domestic Violence in Ireland (SDVII) began life as a hastily scribbled logo drawn by Priscilla as she finalised plans for the new group during a weekend away in Leitrim.

'It was basically a stop sign with a hand in front of it,' laughs Ainie, 'but that's how it started.'

After two years of planning and research, Priscilla and Ainie set up a Facebook page and the new organisation went live on July 7, 2016. The page simply said: 'We are a mother and daughter team. We know the pain you are going through. We are here. Please get in touch.'

Priscilla and Ainie shared the page with all their friends and urged them to do the same.

They tagged other groups, charities, businesses – anyone they could piggy-back to get the word out there.

After a few hours the phone began to ring. And it hasn't stopped ever since.

Ainie was beginning to find her own voice too.

From her ongoing contact with Brian Martin and the team at CDV.org, Ainie understood how being able to talk openly about what she had gone through helped her to heal. She was determined to reach out to other young people who were suffering in silence.

The teenager recognised the huge potential of social media platforms to help get her message across.

Snapchat was her favourite. It allowed users to message her and then delete it straight away without leaving a digital footprint.

In May 2016, Ainie set up her own Snapchat platform; saynotocdv [Say No to Childhood Domestic Violence].

At first it was shared purely through word of mouth.

Ainie found people her age were anxious to talk about their experiences in a safe forum, whether it be mental health issues or domestic abuse.

Gradually, the platform grew and grew. And so did Ainie's confidence. She regularly posted stories about her own experiences and encouraged other to share theirs.

As the numbers grew, Ainie began to reach out to certain influencers and asked them to share her stories on their platforms.

Most of the bloggers were happy to oblige. One of these, James Kavanagh, gave Ainie direct access to a huge new audience on his social media platforms. While she was speaking about her experience of domestic abuse her phone began to bounce. Within 24 hours her story had racked up more than 10,000 views.

Ainie's platform took off like a rocket. She was inundated with calls from people her age with similar stories to her own. Adult victims of domestic abuse also called her to get a better insight into how their own children were affected.

The national media was beginning to take notice too.

In an interview with the Irish Independent published in May 2017, Ainie spoke of the healing impact talking about their experiences can have on young victims.

'On Snapchat I am able to talk about my story, who helped me and then also the different types of abuse that domestic violence includes.

'It's great to be able to help people because I never want to see a man, woman or child go through what I had to go through with domestic violence.'

Ainie spoke openly about attending counselling and therapy, which helped her to cope with anxiety, stress and depression, but said she still experienced flashbacks. And she admitted her abuse had such an effect that at one point she experienced suicidal ideation.

'I wanted to end it all at one point because I couldn't take any more, but I told my mum how I felt and she brought me to see a counsellor who has been a fantastic help.'

More than five years later, Ainie still attends therapy and admits she probably will for the rest of her life. She continues to have regular sessions with her counsellor for anxiety, depression, trauma and PTSD (post-traumatic stress disorder).

She loves her job working at Cassidy Travel, who she says have supported and encouraged her advocacy work.

In the main, Ainie insists she has a happy and fulfilling life, for which she largely credits her mother and granny, along with her regular sessions with her psychiatrist, Dr Miriam Kennedy. But she admits the feelings of sadness and rejection never fully go away.

No child should have to beg their dad, or any parent, to have a relationship. It makes you feel like absolute crap; you feel so unwanted. Rejected.

Even now I'm 24 and I still feel rejected by him, even though I've gone through the mill of it all and come out the other side.

Yeah, I admit, I do long for the idea of having a dad, but it's not him. It's the father figure I'd love to have in my life. My grandad Pat was the only real father figure I've ever had, even though I was just nine when he died.

Obviously, my mam gives me the double of it, but you look at other kids and it is still hurtful now because you're in your twenties and you realise how much you missed out by not really having a dad growing up.

Even when I finished school, I was dying to tell him about my Leaving Cert results or be dying to tell him about friends, you know, so it's sad when it comes to stuff like that. Even without the domestic abuse, when I take that and put it to the side, I always felt like he never wanted me as a child.

———

Despite the benefits of counselling and the confidence she has gained through her advocacy and media work, Ainie admits she still feels 'really vulnerable' when it comes to meeting men.

She said she was drawn into a few 'toxic' relationships that were heading to a dark place before she managed to pull away.

In one of these, an ex-boyfriend became increasingly emotionally and verbally abusive towards her. She said friends tried to warn her about his behaviour, but she was blind to it - until it almost reached the point of physical violence.

'I actually didn't see it at the time, but I was right where my mam was, being emotionally and verbally abused. I just wasn't married to him,' she recalls.

She said the bubble finally burst when, during a heated row, her then boyfriend turned to her and said: 'You want me to hit you, don't you?'

'My whole body froze. I just looked at him and I went; "Seriously? You're coming down to that?" I remember feeling like, "do you know, if he did hit me, it'd probably be easier." So I totally felt, in that position at that time, "that's exactly how my mam used to feel."

'He had an awful temper. It reminds me of dad a lot; a street angel, house devil. When he was in other people's company they'd think, "ah he's lovely." In my head, I was thinking, "You haven't got a clue."'

Afterwards, Ainie says she went from 'the frying pan into the fire'.

She met a guy who 'came from a lovely family' and initially showered her with attention. But as time went on, he became more and more controlling, often putting her down when they were in company to knock her confidence.

'He'd tell me how to dress, what to do with my hair, what colours to wear. One night we were in town and we ended up having a row. I was wearing a pair of leather leggings with boots, and he was like, "they look ridiculous on you."'

'He just put me down to make me feel like a piece of shit.'

There were also signs of financial abuse in her early 'toxic' relationships.

'I must look like a glorified banker ... I'd be thick, I'd be feeling sorry for them having no money. I don't want to see anyone stuck when it comes to money, and I get that from my mam. My mam was the same.'

Now, Ainie says half-jokingly, to protect herself she carries out her own form of 'Garda vetting' on potential partners.

———

I need a CV. If I'm out on a Saturday night and someone is chatting me up, I have an extra layer around me - probably a whole fortress.

I'm like; 'Where are you from? Who's your mam? Who's your dad?'

What they do workwise is a big thing. Like mam, I've become pretty resourceful so I can find out pretty quickly if they're spoofing.

If I'm talking to anyone, I put up a barrier. There are a few things I always look out for, especially drugs and gambling.

Cocaine has become such a huge thing and the drug is fuelling so many cases of domestic violence now, so I look out for that. The signs are usually pretty easy to spot.

Gambling as well. I'd always suss out if they have a Paddy Power or a Boylesports app. If they do it's, 'Sorry, see you later, you're getting blocked.'

If Cheltenham or Fairyhouse is on I'd somehow bring it up in a conversation. They'll either say they're big into it or not interested in that type of thing.

Then there's the controlling behaviour. You often don't see it until you're in the relationship, but there are some tell-tale signs. Like if you're going out on a date and he insists on paying for everything.

I hate people paying for me, but that's just me. I like to be able to say I'm independent and have my own money.

These days Ainie is happy being young, free and single. Occasionally she sees her father driving his taxi around the city, which can be upsetting and reinforce the feelings of rejection she carried into abusive relationships of her own.

But mistakes can make powerful lessons and Ainie, despite everything she has endured, says it's all part of her learning curve.

'I don't want to be stuck down in a relationship at 24 and not explore the world. I regret being in those toxic relationships, but I don't regret learning from them.'

33

March 31, 2020

IT WAS less than a week into lockdown and Priscilla was already feeling the strain.

Her phone hadn't stopped ringing since Taoiseach Leo Varadkar announced sweeping restrictions to slow the spread of coronavirus.

As part of the unprecedented curbs on social and commercial life, people were urged to remain at home, and only venture out to shop for food and exercise briefly within 2km of their residence.

In a televised address from Government Buildings in Dublin on March 27, Mr Varadkar announced a ban on all public or private gatherings and visits to hospitals and prisons, with some exceptions on compassionate grounds.

Meanwhile, people aged over 70 and vulnerable groups were told to 'cocoon' in isolation.

Addressing the nation, Mr Varadkar said: 'I'm appealing to every man, woman and child to make these sacrifices for the love of each other ... show that you care for your family and friends; stay home.

'These are radical actions aimed at saving as many people's lives as possible in the days and weeks ahead.'

The Covid-19 restrictions posed significant challenges for every family in the country. But for victims of domestic violence, the prospect of being couped up with their abuser for 24 hours during lockdown was a genuinely terrifying one.

It wasn't long before frontline organisations such as Stop Domestic Violence in Ireland began to feel the impact.

Just days after the Taoiseach's address, Priscilla was struggling to deal with an upsurge in calls from victims.

———

Within 48 hours [of lockdown coming into effect] there was a significant rise in the number of calls coming through.

Before Covid-19 it already felt as though domestic abuse cases were like a ticking timebomb; now we were seeing the explosions go off.

I got over 50 calls within two days from victims desperately looking for help. In most of these cases the abuser had serious addiction issues; alcoholics, drug and gambling addicts who were now stuck at home without access to pubs, drugs or the bookies. Who do you think they're going to take it out on? Unfortunately, it was almost always their victims, those closest to them and – in many cases – the children who were in the firing line.

The courts were also closed during lockdown, which made it much harder for victims to secure safety, protection and barring orders. Interim barring orders were available, but only in extreme cases. Victims had to be able to prove their life was in severe danger to have a chance of getting one.

———

In Harcourt Street in Dublin, at the headquarters of the Garda National Protective Services Bureau (GNPSB), Chief Superintendent Declan Daly and his team were preparing to unveil the country's policing response to Covid-19.

Operation Faoiseamh, meaning respite, was launched on April 1, just days into the first lockdown,

The World Health Organization (WHO) officially declared the coronavirus outbreak a pandemic on March 11, but even before this senior gardai knew an avalanche of domestic abuse cases was coming down the tracks.

Supt Daly and a team of senior officers at the bureau closely studied the policing response to Covid-19 in other countries and how restrictions were impacting on families and those affected by domestic abuse.

Rather than sit waiting for the calls to come in, Daly and his team decided to take a more proactive approach. They devised a 'traffic light' system to help victims and families affected by domestic violence.

Officers at the GNPSB, which consisted of 245 gardai and staff and 16 Divisional Protective Service Units (DPSUs), began phoning anyone who had previously reported domestic abuse.

Anyone in immediate danger was classified as 'red'. Those who faced a possible but not instant threat were listed as 'amber', while potential victims who did not foresee a danger to their safety were ranked as 'green'.

A senior member of the team involved in the operation said the proactive approach was vital to reassure survivors and potential victims that gardai were there to help.

Before the first cases were confirmed we had already been looking closely at other countries that were, at the start, more advanced in terms of contagion.

We looked at countries such as France and the UK where they were experiencing spikes in domestic abuse, so we knew this was going to happen here. It was clear from other countries and from our own experience what lockdown [meant] … families in a closed environment in a pressure cooker.

We were off the start line early [in terms of response]. Covid really hit us in March – we were up and running by April 1. It was quick, but it needed that response.

It was a stressful time for everybody. The kids are home, there's restrictions on movement. It was a difficult environment.

For most houses these were testing times, but not violent times. But for some people, the victims who are married to an abuser, we recognised it was going to be a violent time and we needed to respond to that.

With [Operation] Faoiseamh, we wanted to ensure there was increased reporting, that the help was there for people who were in trouble.

We went back to people who previously made contact with An Garda Síochána, people who had reported domestic abuse before.

We wrote it down in the form of a traffic light system; red for people who needed our help there and then. And there wasn't a huge amount, thankfully. But there was a lot of ambers and a lot of greens.

You could tell people were relieved that we'd got in touch.

We made the calls. Usually, you sit back and wait for the calls to come in, but we turned it on its head to be more proactive.

Everyone was gearing up for what was coming down the line with different issues around Covid and domestic abuse. The NGOs, particularly the people running refuges, they all knew we were in for a busy time.

———

Just one week into lockdown, Priscilla, Ainie and their network of volunteers and survivors were already struggling to cope with the volume of pleas for help.

This was partly because Stop Domestic Violence in Ireland's own public profile had significantly increased in the months leading up to the pandemic.

The previous summer a play based on Priscilla and Ainie's life, Some Names Were Changed, received standing ovations every night of its week-long run at the Projects Arts Centre as part of the Dublin Fringe Festival. The Ross Dungan scripted play was nominated for Best Production and struck a powerful chord with domestic abuse victims.

In January, a campaign spearheaded by Priscilla, highlighting how rampant cocaine use was fuelling domestic violence cases, featured in almost all national media outlets, in print, broadcast and online. Several regional and local news outlets also covered the story.

In one interview, Priscilla prophetically warned: 'This is just the tip of the iceberg.'

During the first lockdown regime Priscilla found herself fielding more and more calls from victims who had never previously reported abuse. SDVII's media awareness campaigns were having an impact; but

Priscilla and Ainie found themselves more stretched than ever.

They noticed a huge rise in coercive control and financial abuse cases as abusers ruthlessly exploited Covid restrictions to cement their dominance over victims. In one case an abuser burned all his partner's clothes to stop her from leaving.

Many victims were plunged into financial crisis as abusive former husbands and partners withheld maintenance.

In some cases, ex-partners refused to return children to their mother in the knowledge the courts were only open to cater for emergency orders. In most of these instances the mothers were too afraid to go to the father's home without the protection of the courts.

In one case a mother was beaten unconscious after her former partner took their child away from her. Another woman was horrifically tortured and had five of her fingers broken.

Illustrating the growing levels of violence during the first lockdown regime, family law solicitor Sandra McAleer noted: 'The scale and the nature of much of the abuse [during lockdown] was pretty horrific. In one case a woman had a bag put over her head in an attempt to suffocate her.'

Priscilla also noticed a worrying rise in cases involving older people being abused in their own homes as lockdown restrictions exacerbated existing family tensions.

In one case a victim was violently attacked and slammed against a wall, requiring hospital treatment. In another case parents sought a protection order against their adult son who was getting drunk and abusing them in their home.

A growing number of men were also coming forward to SDVII seeking help. Priscilla knew these cases were also just the tip of the iceberg owing to the perceived stigma attached to men trapped in abusive and violent relationships.

The escalating domestic abuse crisis was also fuelling the deepening homeless and housing emergency. Refuges across the country quickly filled up. SDVII began working with housing charities and launched fundraising campaigns to help victims and their children who were forced to flee the family home – in some cases with just the clothes on their backs – and now found themselves homeless.

By June, gardai confirmed a massive 25% year-on-year increase in domestic abuse cases, many of which were reported in the previous three months when restrictions forced many victims to remain in lockdown with their abusers.

SDVII found itself in the eye of an unprecedented domestic abuse storm. Priscilla publicly warned it was only a matter of time before someone was killed in their home.

On April 17, 2021, the remains of a young mother-of-two were discovered at her apartment in Finglas on Dublin's northside.

Jennifer Poole, 24, had been stabbed seven times with a kitchen knife.

Her partner Gavin Murphy, 30, was arrested and later charged with her murder.

Murphy would eventually be given a mandatory sentence of life imprisonment at Dublin's Central Criminal Court. At the murder trial, a neighbour of Jennifer's told how she heard high-pitched screaming 'like never before' coming from her apartment and heard the victim shouting 'stop, please don't do this' over and over.

On the morning of the murder, Priscilla received a tip off about the horrific killing before the news broke in the media. She immediately checked the SDVII database containing details of victims and survivors the group has assisted.

Jennifer's name didn't register. However, it subsequently emerged the suspect had 13 previous convictions, including one for assaulting an ex-partner and another for producing a knife.

A few days after Jennifer's murder, Priscilla sent the Poole family a bouquet of flowers with a short note offering her condolences and any support the group could provide.

Jennifer's brother, Jason Poole, got in touch with Priscilla. He told her the family were absolutely devastated. They simply couldn't understand what could drive somebody to murder their beautiful sister and daughter, and in such a brutal fashion.

Priscilla warned Jason the family faced a very difficult few months ahead.

———

We just tried to let Jason and his family know we were there to provide as much support as we could, but there was no sugar-coating what was coming down the line; the Garda investigation, the media interest, the courts ... their lives would never be the same again.

When it came out that the suspect had a previous conviction for domestic violence Jason connected the dots; Jennifer could still be alive today if her killer had been placed on a register of domestic abusers.

———

Priscila and SDVII had been calling for a national domestic violence register – similar to the Sex Offenders' Register – since the murder of Nadine Lott, the young county Wicklow mother who was brutally beaten to death by her ex, trained boxer Daniel Murtagh, in December 2019.

The huge rise in domestic abuse cases during the pandemic had finally propelled the issue to the top of the political agenda. Politicians from all parties joined a growing chorus of demands for tougher legislation to protect victims and their children.

Long before this Priscilla and Ainie had been calling for a radical overhaul in how the State responds to domestic abuse, including greater supports for victims, enhanced policing resources and family court reforms.

In several media interviews, Priscilla doubled down on her calls for a national database of domestic abusers.

SDVII also called for domestic violence to be made a named crime in its own right, similar to Australia where abusers are given enhanced sentences for offences against victims.

Priscilla argued for the introduction of 'no contact' orders for anyone who feels at risk; stricter sentences for breaches of protection orders and longer jail terms for repeat abusers.

To reflect the upsurge in cases, she also called for every Garda station in the country to have its own dedicated domestic abuse unit staffed with specialist officers.

The scale of the rise in domestic abuse cases throughout the pandemic was laid bare in a report by John Drennan published in the Irish Mail on Sunday on November 2021.

The article – based on figures provided by the Department of Justice in response to queries from Independent TD Michael McNamara – confirmed 33,420 domestic abuse incidents were reported in the first nine months of the year; a rate of almost 1,000 a week.

Gardai received a total of 24,686 calls relating to domestic incidents between January and September 2021.

The Dublin region (8,941) accounted for the highest number of calls.

The Eastern region, consisting of counties Kildare, Kilkenny, Carlow, Laois, Offaly, Meath, Waterford and Westmeath recorded 5,612 incidents. In the Southern Region – including Cork, Clare, Kerry Limerick and Tipperary – 5,030 incidents were reported. Meanwhile, the North-West – comprising Cavan, Monaghan, Donegal, Galway, Louth, Mayo, Roscommon, Longford, Sligo and Leitrim – had 5,103.

The department also confirmed a further 3,188 breaches of court orders – including barring, protection and safety orders – 2,657 of which resulted in charges being brought.

Gardai also recorded 5,364 'other' domestic criminal incidents, which resulted in a further 1,362 charges.

Within Irish law, barring orders serve several different purposes.

A safety order prohibits the abuser from further acts of violence or threats of violence. If the alleged abusive person does not live with the victim, a safety order requires them to stay away from the family home. If both parties live together, the person accused of abuse must undertake not to threaten or assault their partner.

A barring order requires the violent person to leave the family home.

A protection order has the same effect as a safety order and is granted where the court finds an immediate risk to the victim. It remains in place until a court hearing can take place, while an interim barring order requires the abuser to leave home, but lasts no longer than a period of eight days, pending a court hearing.

Commenting on the figures, Mr McNamara said the country was now in the grip of a domestic violence 'epidemic'.

Social Democrats co-leader Catherine Murphy said 'a fundamental change in mind-set' was now needed to tackle the issue.

'It is really concerning to see such high numbers and it follows on from a significant escalation last year of what is described as domestic abuse.

'If a stranger in the street was the offender, would attitudes, including in Government and Law Enforcement, be different?' she asked.

Ms Murphy said using the term 'domestic' categorises abuse in a way 'that removes this abuse as a general threat to society'.

Echoing Michael McNamara's comments, she added: 'We need to see this as an epidemic at this stage and invest appropriately in effective measures to actively reduce the risk to many women, children and men, who face abuse as part of their daily existence.'

Despite the proactive approach taken by An Garda Síochána at the start of the pandemic, the force was later embroiled in a major controversy when it emerged that thousands of emergency calls about domestic violence, missing persons and health concerns were 'cancelled' by officers.

It subsequently emerged one of the cancelled 999 calls was from a woman who had just been raped and feared her attacker was returning.

Another cancelled call was from a woman in Dublin who was being attacked by a man with a weapon and feared for her life.

Priscilla said the 999 calls scandal underlines the need for gardai to be given far greater resources and expertise to tackle domestic abuse. She repeated her call for every Garda station in the country to have its own dedicated and trained senior officer to oversee and coordinate responses to domestic violence.

'It's absolutely clear that gardai do not have the resources and the type of skill set [needed] to combat domestic abusers. I know most gardai are very dedicated and trying to do the best job they can in difficult circumstances, but in many areas, they are being asked to fight a losing battle,' she said in one interview.

'The Government keeps saying "the resources are there" but that's simply not the case. From day to day we can see there is a huge disparity in how different Garda stations and areas are able to deal with domestic abuse cases and that's down to Garda numbers, experience and training.

'In Dublin, due to the population, it's particularly bad because they are dealing with so many other types of crime and, unfortunately, we are still finding that domestic violence cases are often not being prioritised.'

Providing dedicated Garda domestic abuse specialists in every district in the country would involve a significant injection of resources.

Every Garda student participates in 'victim-focused', interactive courses as part of their training at the Garda Síochána College in Templemore. Recruits to the Garda National Protective Services Bureau (GNPSB) also undergo further expert training to police domestic abuse situations.

Each Garda division also has a dedicated active response unit for domestic abuse and specialist services to deal with more serious cases.

Frontline services deal with the majority of cases, but if there's a complex element to the case it will most likely be investigated by the GNPSB.

Senior security sources argue it is not feasible to only have specialist gardai dealing with domestic abuse and point to the 40,000 incidents reported in 2021.

One top ranking officer who spent decades policing domestic abuse cases in Ireland said: 'Every member of An Garda Síochána is trained to deal with incidents as they arise.

'There will be cases where specialisation is needed to step in – and that's there – but it can't be just the one specialist unit dealing with that. 'They [specialist officers] have rest days, they've got holidays ... so you're not getting the best value for your money for that.

'The fact of the matter is, though, there is no magical solution when it comes to policing domestic abuse.

'It's an extremely difficult crime to investigate and to deal with because it's about control.

'This is a crime that is, for the most point, behind closed doors. It can be very complex. A robbery is visible; in the shop there will be CCTV cameras, there's witnesses. Domestic abuse takes place at home or behind closed doors; it's not visible to the public and it's only when somebody takes the brave step to report it that it becomes visible.

'At the end of the day, you're trying to address human culture, which has an element of violence.'

The Domestic Violence Act [2018] made coercive control a criminal offence and gave gardai significant extra powers and scope to police domestic abuse.

Before the legislation, when gardai were called to a domestic violence incident they were just dealing with an assault. Now, they can examine controlling, coercive and threatening behaviour and other forms of domestic abuse, including financial and emotional abuse.

But while the Domestic Violence Act gave gardai greater leeway to bring abusers to justice, the severely backlogged courts were buckling under the weight of the soaring domestic abuse case load.

34

THE YOUNG man shuffled into the courtroom in handcuffs flanked by four gardai.

He was unshaven and bleary-eyed after spending a night in prison for repeatedly ignoring court orders to pay maintenance.

More than six months earlier a bench warrant was issued for his arrest after he was served with a penal warning. He continued to ignore repeated warnings to provide for his young children while his maintenance debt soared to more than €20,000.

His dark coloured jeans and jacket matched his mood. Despite all the warnings it was clear he hadn't been expecting to spend the night in a cell courtesy of the taxpayer.

The respondent's solicitor was first out of the traps.

His client, he told the judge, was 'disappointed' at being brought into the court 'in chains'. He also suffered the indignity of being given a teabag during his overnight stay, but no cup.

The lawyer said his client had received a job offer and was prepared to 'immediately' commence paying €50 a week, adding he hoped to be in a position to increase this to €150 once he started work.

The solicitor representing the respondent's former partner offered a different perspective.

'There is a credibility issue here,' she told the court. 'He hasn't paid a penny for months,' she added, calling for a statement of means and two years' bank statements to be provided to the court.

The judge hearing the case ordered the respondent be released from custody but warned him: 'I hope a salutary lesson has been learned.'

This remains to be seen. Since his last court date, the young father has made an attempt to make some maintenance payments, but not the amount promised to the court. The outstanding lump sum remains unpaid.

The brief hearing, which was over in a matter of minutes, is typical of many of the thousands of family law cases coming before the backlogged Dublin District Family Court in the heart of Temple Bar every month.

Outside on the street, throngs of tourists pass by Dolphin House, the distinctive four-storey Victorian building, which was previously a hotel, oblivious to the often-harrowing tales of human suffering unfolding inside.

In another case, a young mother was opposing an application by her former partner, sitting directly across from her dressed in a smart navy-blue suit, for joint custody of their 11-year-old daughter.

Giving evidence, the mother told how she withdrew access to their daughter when she returned home upset after staying with her father. The girl said her father verbally abused her and pinched her, causing her to cry.

Her mother also said her ex was violent towards her during their relationship. She said that when she confronted him about his behaviour, he became angry and abusive. The mother became emotional as she outlined her reasons for opposing access, telling the judge: 'It's my job as a mother to protect her.'

Giving evidence later, her former partner insisted he had an 'incredible relationship' with his daughter. He denied shouting or being aggressive towards her and apologised to his ex for the way 'I behaved towards you' during their relationship.

He accepted he had criminal convictions and promised to undergo any necessary counselling or courses the court felt necessary, 'anything, anything to see my child again'.

The case, which had already been rumbling through the Covid congested family court system for almost three years, ran over and was adjourned yet again, much to the frustration of the mother.

Earlier her solicitor complained that her client's former partner had a history of making 'vexatious applications' to the court which had delayed the case.

In one of the consultation rooms on the first floor of Dolphin House, a mother-of-two is anxiously waiting for her case to be recalled.

The previous week her husband breached a court safety order when he scaled a wall into the back garden and threw a large brick through the window of the door, shattering the glass and sending shards across the full length of the kitchen.

Her two terrified sons were upstairs when their father smashed his way through the back door. The older boy got up and ran outside to his neighbour's house and got them to call the gardai.

The local Garda station was only a short distance away, but it took the officers 30 minutes to get to the scene, where they found the abuser drunkenly roaring at his wife and two boys.

It took the gardai several minutes to subdue the man, but they eventually managed to bundle him into the back of the squad car. He was taken to the Garda station where he was formally charged with breaching the court order and taken into custody.

In a written application for a barring order against his father, the older son told how he longer 'felt safe in my house'. He said his father threatened to kill him and that for the past two months his little brother 'has been sleeping with knives by his bedside he's that scared'.

In a separate application, the boys' mother said her sons were 'traumatised' by their father's 'out of control' behaviour. They now 'live on edge', she wrote, living in fear of 'what he'll do next'.

Seven days after the incident his wife returned to Dolphin House where she was making an application for a long-term barring order against her husband. She was very nervous; her first experience at the family court two months earlier was not a pleasant one. She did succeed in securing a safety order on that occasion, but only after a gruelling hour and a half hearing during which she felt as if she was the one on trial.

———

It was an extremely traumatic experience. It was my first time in the court and I didn't know what to expect. He [abuser] walks in and gives me the look – do you know how intimidating that is?

So now I have to sit in court with this absolute monster that's being abusing me for years and has now started on my children.

I was trying to explain to the judge why I needed him out of the house, but it just felt as if the judge didn't get it.

I was a nervous wreck standing there trying to explain. He'd smashed in my door after being out on a bender all weekend and the youngest lad was asking 'where's dad?'.

I texted him saying I was locking up the house at 11pm. He rolls in at 5am in the morning and smashed the door down because he's too drunk to put the key in the door. I was trying to explain this to the judge, but he told me I had 'intent' to lock him out of the home because of the text.

I could feel myself falling apart. I was trying to stress to the judge that he had his own keys – that he wasn't locked out of the house – and he's sitting across from me loudly muttering 'lies, lies' while I was speaking.

It took me three years before I eventually had the courage to leave him and this was my first time in the family court, and it was pure hell. I can understand why so many victims are afraid to get out when this is what they have to face.

Surely there are ways domestic violence victims can be made to feel safer in court. Why do we have to be in the same room as our abuser? The technology is there, why can't it be done by video link?

I felt extremely intimidated. I know I was saying all the words wrong, nothing would come out right I was so nervous.

I was in there for an hour and a half – it felt like a lifetime.

Two months later the mother-of-two was back in the family court. She felt a bit stronger now but prayed the matter would be dealt with swiftly. She had to get the day off work to attend the hearing and was grateful she had an understanding boss.

Shortly before 11am her case was called but then quickly adjourned amid confusion over whether or not gardai had served the barring order to her husband. She didn't even know if her husband was still in prison or back on the streets. His car was still parked outside her house. Her older son was away on a school trip, but her younger boy was due to return home from school in a few hours.

She stayed in one of the consultation rooms on the first floor of the courthouse waiting to see if her case would be called again. She was too afraid to go downstairs to the reception area on her own in case her husband was there.

In the adjourning room, a six-week-old baby whose mother was seeking a barring order against the child's father cried constantly. Outside in the hallway, an elderly man with severe cuts and bruising to the left side of his face sat in a daze waiting for his case to be called.

Every few minutes a cheerful, English accented voice boomed from the court intercom, concisely enunciating case numbers as if he was picking bingo balls out of a drum.

'Final call for 1092 of 2021, SD and LMcD to Court 47 on the first floor please.'

While she waited, the mother called the local Garda station to see if they could shed any light on her husband's whereabouts, but to no avail.

Shortly after lunch, her barrister confirmed he had been released from jail, but it was still unclear if he had been served with the barring order.

Finally, at 4.17pm her case was called. This time the hearing was mercifully swift, but inconclusive. It emerged the 12-month barring order had been served to her husband, but the signed Declaration of Service had not been presented to the court. As a result, the judge could only issue an interim seven-day barring order. The victim would have to return to court again the following week and go through the whole experience all over again.

Priscilla Grainger said her group is seeing an increasing number of cases in which gardai fail to serve orders on abusers; a situation she claims is placing victims' lives in danger.

———

This is becoming a big problem and something that needs to be addressed before someone is killed.

Just today I've had to send letters to four separate Garda stations relating to barring orders that were not served on the abuser.

In one case the victim, who was very badly beaten up, is now in hiding while two interim barring orders have not been served on her abuser.

It has taken a huge amount of courage for her to come to the realisation that her life is in danger and that she needs to get out. She shouldn't have had to seek a second interim order at all because the first one wasn't served.

I've written a letter to the Garda Commissioner Drew Harris to highlight the matter, but it's something that needs to be addressed – and now – before we find ourselves dealing with yet another domestic murder.

Located on East Essex Street directly across the street from the fashionable Clarence Hotel, Dolphin House deals with domestic violence cases along with guardianship, maintenance payments and access issues. Just inside the door and up 10 steps is a jaded looking reception and waiting area with rows of orange coloured seats. Posters adorn the walls with contact numbers for emergency refuges and domestic violence services. There are five courtrooms in the building along with a small number of consultation rooms.

Abuse survivors insist Dolphin House is completely unsuitable for victims of domestic violence – who often find themselves almost cheek to jowl with their abusers inside the cramped family court.

In one recent incident Priscilla attended the court with a victim who was seeking a protection order against her former partner.

The victim didn't think he would turn up at the court and shot Priscilla a nervous look when he walked into the reception area. As soon as he spotted his ex the man walked towards her, making an intimidating hissing noise as he passed.

Priscilla stood up, using a folder as a kind of makeshift shield above the terrified woman while she alerted an officer at reception.

He only moved off because I stood up to him and the Garda ordered him to move to the other side of the room.

I've seen this type of scenario play out time and time again and it clearly illustrates how our family law courts are not fit for purpose when it comes to dealing with domestic violence cases.

The court staff are always very kind and have a lovely way about them, but it can be a very frightening place for victims. Can you imagine how hard it is to have the courage to walk away from your abuser, and then having to face them staring over at you in a small room while you're waiting for your case to be heard?

In August, an article by investigative journalist Ken Foxe published details of a consultation report on a planned new €100m family law complex to replace Dolphin House.

Echoing survivors' concerns, the report found the country's cramped law courts can be 'intimidating spaces' with very little privacy for domestic abuse victims.

Judges and court staff also complained about the potential for 'intimidation and aggression from the public' at entrances, reception areas and in routes around the buildings.

'Waiting areas can become a flash point for intimidation by the other party and their agents when making a domestic violence order,' the report stated.

Judges also raised 'significant concerns' about the layout of the proposed new family court complex at Hammond Lane, just across the River Liffey in Smithfield.

However, Priscilla and several family law experts believe a more radical solution is needed to ensure domestic violence victims feel safe in our courts.

Given the unique and highly sensitive nature of cases, Priscilla insists a dedicated court is needed to deal solely with domestic abuse issues.

'Victims should not have to go into a courthouse and have their abuser eyeball them. There needs to be a separate area, a separate meeting room where victims and their children are looked after.

'Aside from providing far greater protection, a dedicated domestic abuse court would also significantly speed up cases and prevent the type of backlog we are seeing now in family courts. For example, when a victim is leaving court with their barring order, it needs to be served immediately – not two days or two weeks later.'

The backlog in domestic abuse cases is exacerbated by a shortage of judges.

The impact of this was clearly visible during a visit to Dolphin House one Thursday in mid-September. The reception area downstairs was packed with anxious partners waiting for their cases to be called. Occasionally, tensions boiled over.

One woman had to be forcibly removed from the downstairs area by gardai after she became abusive to staff.

Family law solicitor Sandra McAleer, who has been attending the court since 2006, said it is being overwhelmed with domestic abuse cases.

'The difficulty is the lack of judges – this is the third time this week we've only had three in a full court sitting. It's been a problem since September 2021.

'The level of domestic violence cases is way beyond the level when I started practising family law. It's unbelievable. Just looking at my list of 50 cases this week; almost every one of them has some element of domestic abuse attached to it. There hasn't been a single day I've come here for the past two years where there wasn't a case of domestic violence - it's huge. We are still backlogged [after Covid-19] and it's a huge backlog. Covid did affect everyone, especially couples that may have already been on the rocks [before the pandemic hit]. There was a lot of separations, a lot of domestic violence cases where people were stuck together with no schools, no third parties, no escape from bad situations ... and to a pretty scary level.'

Ms McAleer admits the increasingly brutal nature of some of the attacks is concerning. She rattles off a spate of horrific recent incidents off the top of her head. Partners beaten up and locked up for hours. Women being stabbed. In one case a victim's fingers were hacked off.

Ms McAleer says drug use, particularly cocaine, is fuelling many domestic violence cases.

'Cocaine is a major issue – you see it in a lot of attacks. Some really terrible things ... and a lot of it being done in front of children. People don't seem to care about arguing in front of children anymore.'

Solicitors, court staff and even judges are not immune to the violence.

In December 2015, family law judge Justice Miriam Walsh was attacked in her courtroom at Dolphin House and beaten for up to a minute before gardai managed to restrain her assailant. All the courtrooms in Dolphin House now have panic buttons installed for the judges' protection.

Ms McAleer says she is physically threatened 'all the time' in course of her work.

'There was one guy - he was the ex-partner of a woman I was acting on behalf of - who waited for me to come out of court and followed me calling me every name under the sun, but I don't allow them to intimidate me.

'I had a case where one man brought a lady up to the Dublin Mountains to kill her, but she jumped out of a moving car and got picked up by two Canadians. It went to court – he's in prison at the moment – and in the middle of the barring application he told me "I know where you live" and that I was next to be brought up to the mountains. And this was in court, in front of a judge.'

But she adds: 'He's still in prison, and I'm still here.'

Frank Crummy, a founder member of Ireland's first family planning clinic who has been campaigning on women's issues for seven decades, says a 24-hour emergency court is needed to deal with increasingly violent domestic abuse cases.

The 83-year-old, who also played a key role setting up the country's first refuge for women, has plenty of experience dealing with the type of extremely violent cases he says require immediate court attention.

'Lots of cases just can't wait – they need to be dealt with straight away.'

The diminutive campaigner is himself no stranger to violence. He received several beatings at the hands of abusive husbands as he tried to protect women in the refuge, the stress of which eventually caused him to have a nervous breakdown.

'I remember having to jump between a woman and her husband while he was trying to knife her.

'Another time I pulled up outside the refuge on Harcourt Road and a husband was trying to kick down the front door. I ran over and just as I was getting to him the door pushed in. He went in and I ran after him. I grabbed him around the legs and pulled him down and he kicked the shite out of me. He was 6ft 4.'

Campaigners and legal experts are also calling for expert training to be provided to judges, barristers, solicitors and gardai dealing with domestic violence cases.

Veteran legal executive David Ivers, who Priscilla said provides 'invaluable' advice to her support group in helping victims to prepare their cases before they go to court, said: 'In many cases the expertise for dealing with these cases is not there. I don't mean any disrespect to any of my colleagues, but the fact is that a lot of these have not practised domestic abuse law and they don't understand domestic violence.'

Sandra McAleer agrees. 'There should be training for everyone when it comes to domestic violence, not just the judges. The guards, solicitors, barristers – all advocates of the law – should have specialist training.

'At the moment judges get no training at all in terms of domestic violence, they're just going by their own instinct and intelligence on whether or not someone is telling the truth.

'But a lot of people using the family courts lie, so I'm not sure how effective swearing on the oath actually is. It's contempt of court. If people are lying on oath, they should be found in contempt of court.'

Priscilla has also publicly called for judges and legal practitioners dealing with domestic violence to receive expert training.

———

There are criminal solicitors who have no experience of family law dealing with cases who don't have the expertise they need. A big issue is the payment for legal aid is so low, so this needs to be reviewed.

Unfortunately, the court system in place to deal with domestic violence is no longer fit for purpose. We need a dedicated domestic violence court, specialist training and much better enforcement of safety, protection and barring orders.

As we are seeing from the scale and sheer brutality of many domestic violence cases today, society is changing. But the system is not changing with it.

The State needs to adapt and quick, because the problem on the ground is just getting worse and worse.

Unfortunately, it usually takes a major tragedy before the political will is there to do something.

———

35

CALLS for political action to protect women reached a crescendo following the killing of Ashling Murphy, who was attacked and killed as she was jogging along a canal towpath in broad daylight outside Tullamore on January 12, 2022.

While the 23-year-old primary school teacher and musician was not a victim of domestic violence, her killing sparked a massive outpouring of grief and anger on social and in traditional media, echoing the reaction in the UK to the murder of 33-year-old Sarah Everard, who was kidnapped and killed by a police officer as she walked home from a friend's house.

Thousands gathered at candlelit vigils across Ireland and in cities around the world to remember Ashling as the Government came under increasing pressure to act.

Messages accompanying floral tributes outside Dáil Éireann demanded a whole of society response to violence against women.

'Everyone has a role to play in undressing violence against women,' one read.

'Why do women have to fight so hard for change?' asked another.

Summing up the groundswell of public anger, Priscilla Grainger said in an interview at the time: 'This awful, awful killing has really struck a chord with people, in particular women who have suffered abuse and violence.'

Priscilla also upped the ante on Government, saying Ashling's killing underlined the need for tougher sentencing for abusers convicted in the courts.

In an open letter to Justice Minister Helen McEntee on social media, she wrote: 'As long as these killers, abusers and perpetrators know how lenient the justice system is they will continue to offend and murder.'

Helen McEntee was already working on a new strategy she promises will radically bolster the Government's response to domestic, sexual and gender based violence.

Addressing the Dáil on January 19, the minister said there would be a 'zero tolerance' approach to violence and abuse against women.

'In Ashling, we see our sisters, our daughters and our mothers.

'In her family, we see our own.

'And as women, we see ourselves and feel an anger and fear that is all too familiar.

'I am sure I was not alone in this House this week in having cried for Ashling, but also for Urantsetseg Tserendorj and Jastine Valdez, and Ana Kriegel and Nadine Lott, and so many others.

'That is why we stand in solidarity and anger, but also in quiet determination.

'That is why we must all work together to achieve a shared goal of zero tolerance of violence and abuse against women.'

While stressing the solutions 'will not come from legislation alone,' the minister promised to enact a series of legislative reforms before the end of the year to protect women and victims of domestic abuse.

These included:

* A new Garda Power Bill to bolster police powers of search, arrest and detention;

* A Digital Recordings Bill to allow for enhanced Garda use of modern technology to investigate serious crimes;

* A law to introduce new criminal offences for stalking and non-fatal strangulation;

* A new provision to allow victims 'in very serious cases' to apply for orders to prevent alleged abusers from communicating with them before trial;

* A new Hate Crimes Bill with enhanced penalties for crimes motivated by prejudice, including gender;

* A new Sexual Offences Bill that will extend victims' anonymity and legal representation for survivors;

* A Sex Offenders Bill to 'strengthen the management and monitoring of sex offenders in the community'.

Ms McEntee said she was also signing an order to bring in new legislation to provide pre-trial hearings to 'significantly improve the trial process for victims of sexual offence'. She also vowed to take 'further measures if needed'.

Speaking directly to survivors, the minister said: 'I know that for victims, coming forward to report what is happening to you is the hardest decision to make.

'There is a responsibility on all of us, as a State, to protect you when you do look for our help.

'By ensuring there is a refuge space for anyone who needs one.

'By supporting more women to live safely in your home if that is your choice.

'By reassuring victims they will be treated with dignity and respect by the criminal justice system.

'Through Supporting A Victim's Journey, my plan to help victims and vulnerable witnesses in sexual violence cases, we are making progress.

'And while this is not simply a criminal justice issue, as Minister for Justice I want to be clear; I will do whatever it takes to ensure that perpetrators are investigated, prosecuted and face the full rigours of the law. That the punishment matches the crime. And that our gardai have sufficient resources and technology and that our laws are strong enough to bring abusers to justice.'

However, Ms McEntee stressed legislation alone is not enough to address domestic abuse and that 'societal and cultural change' is also required. In a plea to men, she added: 'We cannot do this without you. We need you to stand with us. We can make this change and make this moment count.'

In late June the Government formally approved Minister McEntee's new €363m strategy to tackle domestic, sexual and gender-based violence.

She said the implementation plan containing 144 actions – including tougher penalties for abusers and a doubling of refuge places – would be implemented before the end of 2023.

The rising scale of domestic violence was starkly illustrated in a recent Garda review of crime trends which found most murders in Ireland in 2021 were motivated by domestic abuse.

The review, published in late September 2022, also found sexual offences involving domestic abuse increased four-fold the previous year, and that women are now more likely to be targeted in the home.

Of the 25 murders recorded in Ireland in 2021, no fewer than 13 (52%) were linked to domestic abuse. And while murder rates have dropped over time, gardai noted this is the first time in the years analysed since 2013 that domestic abuse has been linked to the majority of murders.

In 2021 there were 817 sex crimes with a domestic abuse motivation reported compared to 205 offences the previous year. The figure represented a massive 399pc increase and accounted for a quarter of all sexual offences reported in 2021.

On average gardaí respond to between 120 and 150 domestic abuse incidents every day, the review found.

Sara Parsons, principal officer with the Garda Analysis Service, noted domestic abuse cases spiked during the Covid-19 lockdowns, but said it was 'striking' these incidents have continued at a higher level following the easing of restrictions, unlike other crimes.

Priscilla said she is 'alarmed, but not surprised' by the rise in reported domestic abuse cases, which broadly tallies with her experience working on the frontline with survivors.

She supports Ms McEntee's legislative reforms and the minister's call for a whole-of-society approach to combat domestic abuse, but the advocate and campaigner believes there are still too many 'cracks in the system' for victims to fall through.

———

The new laws make sense and we welcome them, but the fact is that existing legislation is not being enforced to the level it should be. Every day we see cases in which victims are not being communicated with properly and gardai not serving orders on abusers. The courts are completely backlogged and justice delayed is very often justice denied.

As the latest Garda statistics illustrate, there also needs to be a greater drive to tackle the underlying causes of domestic violence, and not just the effects. We need earlier intervention; programmes in our schools, education campaigns, far better awareness of the signs and indications of domestic violence if we are to finally break the cycle of abuse destroying future generations.

Look, I'm under no illusions, it won't ever be possible to eradicate domestic violence; unfortunately, it's a very sad fact of life for many, many families.

But it's also no longer a taboo subject and the bravery of so many survivors who have taken the step to leave their abusers and speak out about their experiences has finally lifted the veil that shrouded domestic abuse for so long.

Minister's McEntee's reforms are a significant step in the right direction; but these legislative initiatives must be backed by political will on the ground and a wider drive within society to stamp out tolerance of any form of domestic abuse.

If we face this challenge head on now, we could spare many of our children and grandchildren from the abuse and violence that have destroyed so many lives.

But from the indications we are seeing on the ground, things are likely to get worse before they get better.

There are still so many victims hiding in the shadows, too afraid to seek out the help they need to get safe.

We need to do absolutely everything in our power to show them the full support and weight of the State is there waiting to help them – and their children – when they are ready to take their first steps to freedom.

36

November 1, 2022

PRISCILLA WAS already awake, dozing somewhere between sleep and slumber, when the first text of the morning came through at 6.33am.

It began like most of the others.

'Hi – I follow you and your daughter. I need help.'

Priscilla texted the same response she has given to hundreds to victims trapped in similar circumstances.

'Don't worry, I'm here. We will help you.'

It was a pretty typical start to her day.

Victims of domestic violence usually text or message via WhatsApp as their calls are often monitored by their abuser. And when they do reach out for help it's more often early in the morning or late at night when their abuser is asleep.

Priscilla usually wakes at 6.30am. Then its straight onto the phone; checking texts and emails, responding to emergency cases, dispensing whatever legal information or practical advice she can give.

She rarely gets a full night of uninterrupted sleep, but never lets a cry for help go unanswered. She understands the helplessness of feeling alone, the isolation and fear that no one is out there.

On top of the psychological and mental scares, many domestic abuse victims also suffer long term health consequences.

Priscilla has an autoimmune condition caused by the stress and tension of living under the control of her abuser. Occasionally she finds her concentration lapses and she has to lie down for an hour or two to recharge. She also suffers from a debilitating and frequently painful eye condition called uvetis, hair loss and – like many survivors – weight gain. All are directly or indirectly linked to the abuse she suffered.

Priscilla got out of her bed in her mother's old back bedroom at 8.30am. Ann, now 78, lives in a nursing home nearby but visits at least four times a week. Although confined to a wheelchair, the iron lady has lost none of her mental sharpness or wit and speaks to her daughter and granddaughter every day.

Priscila dressed and braced herself for the day ahead.

The family home on the Navan Road is now a thriving guesthouse, catering for up to 17 guests at a time. Ainie still lives in the cabin at the back of the house.

By the time Priscilla was up some of her staff were already busy preparing breakfast.

Priscilla got a brief glimpse of her daughter as Ainie dashed passed her in the doorway.

'Love you mam,' she called back as Priscilla watched her leave, like a little hurricane bellowing her way out the door to her job in the city centre, where she works as a cruise consultant for a travel agency.

Priscilla smiled to herself and allowed herself a mother's indulgence. She is very proud of her daughter and the young woman Ainie has become; strong, independent, caring – and someone, like her mother these days, who doesn't suffer fools gladly.

'I love you too,' she said, but Ainie was already halfway down the driveway and out of earshot.

Priscilla turned her attention to the day job; checking invoices, paying bills, preparing wages, finalising orders.

After grabbing a quick bite for lunch, Priscilla got into the car and headed to the warehouse in Cabra where her friend Mick Weafer was waiting to help her with deliveries of donations for victims.

Christmas seemed to come even quicker this year, she thought ruefully as she reflected on the organised chaos her life had become in the decade since she finally broke free of her abuser.

The van was already there; packed from floor to ceiling with toys, clothes, hampers – anything that would help ease some of stress victims feel as Christmas approaches.

Priscilla and Ainie personally hate Christmas and all the memories it triggers. But they use the festive season to ramp up donation appeals and help victims and their families as much as they can.

Priscilla says Christmas is always the busiest time of the year for the group.

———

At Christmas there's more drinking, drug taking and gambling, which obviously throws more fuel onto abusive relationships.

It's generally a happy time for families, but it's usually the opposite for people in abusive and violent situations.

This year [2022] has been our busiest yet, but we're delighted because it shows victims increasingly have the courage to reach out. Hopefully the message is getting out there.

It's a very difficult time for survivors. A Christmas song came on the radio this morning and I had to leave the kitchen, just to compose myself. It always brings it back. I used to be sick to the pit of my stomach with worry and nerves.

I remember every year you'd be walking on eggshells, trying to anticipate the moods and the eruptions.

I'd be so disappointed for Ainie; not being able to give her the Christmas she deserved. All the horrible things she had to hear and see.

It always comes flooding back when the decorations start going up.

The fear. What am I going to do? Where am I going to get money to put dinner on the table? How will I heat the house?

Some years, out of spite, he wouldn't fill the oil tank – he did everything in his power to destroy what should have been a time filled with happy, magical memories.

I still remember the dread, the pressure ... my hands are sweating thinking about it.

Stop Domestic Violence in Ireland does not accept any cash donations, just vouchers for food, clothes, toys or any of the basics that families need to get them through Christmas.

Aside from donations, Priscilla also personally purchases dozens of mobile phones every year to help women and men who are trying to escape their abusers. The pay-as-you-go phones are basic models, but they're brand new, have their own sim and provide a vital tool to help survivors to break free and access the help they need.

In recent years, especially since the Covid lockdowns, Priscilla has seen a significant rise in financial abuse cases, where the abuser exerts power over their victim by controlling their money – something she is all too familiar with.

Solicitor Sandra McAleer said financial abuse is also increasingly common in domestic abuse cases coming before the courts.

'Financial abuse is a very controlling element of domestic violence,' she explains. 'An abuser doesn't have to physically hit their victims; they can control them financially by drip feeding them small amounts of money for the most basic things, like food for children.

'To exercise control, the abuser has to see where everything is going, where the victim is spending the money. If the abuser can access your bank account, they can pretty much see where you've been in the morning, where you go to at night.'

After signing off on the deliveries, Priscilla checked her phone again. There was a message from a young mother who recently reached out to her.

It was one the most disturbing cases of coercive control Priscilla has ever come across.

Her husband, a senior executive of a well-known company, controls every aspect of his wife's life and finances.

Her hair must be worn as he likes it.

He exerts complete control over food and her eating; she's not allowed to put on weight but is forbidden from wearing skinny jeans. She's also not allowed to cook or go shopping for groceries. No fast food of any description is allowed in the house.

He doesn't allow his wife to touch the washing machine or use the dishwasher. Even the printer is out of bounds.

The businessman also controls every cent his wife spends. There are no bills in her name, and she is given a tiny allowance for 'housekeeping'.

On the rare occasions his wife leaves the house, he warns her: 'You're being recorded.' He has also told her their home is 'bugged'.

When she plucked up the courage to ask him for a divorce, he told her to 'fuck off and be homeless' and threatened to take the children away.

Like so many before her, Priscilla is trying to help the terrified woman to take the first steps to escape her abuser. But in many cases, as it was with Priscilla, it can take several attempts before victims can finally break free.

Priscilla says many victims have no idea of the supports available to them because they have lived such sheltered lives under the shadow of their abuser.

————

You've got to remember; these people have been chipped away at non-stop, from early morning until late at night, 24 hours a day, seven days a week.

They're afraid to make the break and they need reassurance. Money is a huge factor; many believe they can't afford to leave their abuser.

For example, this is one exchange I had today. [Reads out texts]

Victim: 'I've got my abuser out, but I still love him. Should I take him back?'
Priscilla: 'Have you got a safety order in place?'
Victim: 'Yes.'
Priscilla: 'Why do you want to take him back?'
Victim: 'Because I'm weak.'
Priscilla: 'Why are you weak?'
Victim: 'Because I've been let go from my job and I need to take him back to pay the mortgage.'
Priscilla: 'Have you gone to your community officer?'
Victim: 'No – who is that?'
Priscilla: 'Have you gone to social welfare?'
Victim: 'No ... how can they help?'

So, you can see what's happening here. At 7am this lady was going to take back her abuser, mostly for financial reasons. She was going to take him back because she was scared the mortgage wouldn't be paid and that she could lose her home.

By the time she spoke to us at 8.30am she discovered she has other options.

Now she realises she has the support of a community welfare officer and that there are other supports out there to help her.

Many victims simply don't know how to access the supports that are available to them.

We give all the information they're entitled to, and we support them in any way we can. We also have an in-house solicitor who is on hand to provide expert legal advice.

The family court process can be long and hard for survivors, so they need that legal and emotional support.

We direct them to counselling, give them food if they're hungry and clothe them ... anything we can do to give them back the safety and security they're entitled to.

———

By the time Priscilla got home from the warehouse she was exhausted.

Throughout the day she fielded calls from her network of media contacts about various ongoing cases and campaigns.

Awareness of their work has increased as the issue of domestic abuse has moved closer to the top of the political and news agenda.

Priscilla and Ainie have become regular guests and contributors at public events and on national television and radio programmes. Their work on behalf of victims has featured in every national newspaper and most regional media outlets.

The combined pressures of running and living in a busy guesthouse and her advocacy work invariably takes a toll on Priscilla, but increasingly she allows herself an hour or two of downtime in the evening when things are quieter.

She was just emerging from a nap when she heard Ainie come in the door from work. As with most days, they quickly brought each other up to speed with the various cases they dealt with during the day. Despite having a full-time job, Ainie also fields regular calls and requests for help.

They chatted over dinner; one of the ready-made meals Priscilla orders in from a catering company for their guests. Priscilla and Ainie rarely have time to cook, and meals are usually grabbed on the run. But on weekends Priscilla brings her mother and daughter out for a meal, one of the rare occasions when they can relax together away from the house.

———

My mother is a huge part of our lives; only for her we wouldn't be where we are today, in every sense. We owe everything to her.

The house gets fairly chaotic. Lots of people – guests, staff, survivors – coming in and out and we've a good few friends who pop in fairly regularly.

Sometimes the phone can be draining, but recently I've started to lie down for an hour or two in the evening when things are a bit calmer and recharge my batteries.

I've had to because of my health. My biggest fear is that something would happen to me because of the trauma and the stress. I've had a huge amount of tests done over the past few months but thank God everything has been clear so far.

———

At 9pm Priscilla called it a night. She kissed Ainie and went to bed.

Sleep, as usual, does not come easy, but Priscilla didn't mind – it usually takes two hours before she nods off. In the meantime, she was happy just to be horizontal and allow her body to relax.

But her mind was still racing, devising new ideas and strategies for the group and her business.

There are usually more calls for help. It can be stressful at times, but Priscilla admits helping others gives her great satisfaction and 'it's like therapy for me as well to be honest'.

In the cabin outside, Ainie kicked off her shoes and collapsed onto her duvet.

She propped up her pillows and, without thinking, began scrolling through her phone and messages, subconsciously ticking off some boxes in her mind that would need to be opened in the morning.

Finally, she allowed her body and mind to wind down and began browsing through Netflix in search of some light entertainment.

It was shortly after 10.30pm when the sound of another text pinged on her phone.

Ainie read the message and began to type.

'Don't worry, I'm here. We will help you.'

ACKNOWLEDGEMENTS:

Priscilla and **Ainie Grainger** would like to sincerely thank Shane Doran, Paula Forde and Paul Lynch, who helped us to get back on our feet, both financially and emotionally; Pauline Morrison Baynes; Mary and Dermot Hughes; Richard and Josephine Grainger; Hugh and the late Anne Grainger; Mick McCaffrey; Bertie Ahern; Jessica Kate Jacques; Cllr Christy Burke; Liz Marsh; Late Cllr Anthony Flynn; The Flynn and Hanney family; Mick and Tina Weafer; David Ivers; Cian Ivers; Orla Ivers; Columb Fortune, BL; Declan Daly; Colette Flynn and Tom Plant; Gerry and Colette Browne; Deirdre, Brighid and all the McLaughlin family; Tina Beatty and all the staff of Leitrim Lodge Dublin B&B; Wayne and Barry Beatty; Rebecca Kelly of @everywherewegopodcast; Paul Gray; Marian Fulham; Superintendent Finbarr Murphy; Paul Goskar; Consultants Paul Connell and Mr Duncan Rodgers and all the team at the Mater Hospital Eye Department & Mater Private Hospital; Sandra McAleer; Margaret Farrelly, BL; Declan O Boyle; Marty McCleary; Geraldine and Joe Mooney; Philip and Fiona Duffy; Dr. Miriam Kennedy; Cassidy Travel; Amy McKenna; Cara Murphy; Clodagh Walsh; Orla Walsh; Darren May; Ashfield College; Keith Ward; Adrian Kennedy; Jeremy Dixon; Al Foran; James Kavanagh Holly; Bobby, Alfie and Bella Grainger (our bodyguards and best friends!); Susan and Howie Murtagh; Denise Zahirović; Denise O'Rourke; Philip McCaffrey; Kevin Rowe Events; Ross Dungan; Manus Halligan; Matthew Smyth; Ronan Phelan; John Cronin; Michael Bellew, of Farrelly Dawe White; AIB Dame Street; Ken Kirwan of Little Poppy

Design Marketing; SKMarketing; Brady Management Global; Karen Morgan; Marty McCleary; Maureen Looney.

Shane Doran would like to thank: my wife Laura for her unwavering support, encouragement and patience, and to Michael Wolsey for his wisdom, advice and peerless editing skills. I am grateful to everyone who shared their valuable time, insights and expertise; to Deirdre, Brighid and all the McLaughlin family, Bertie Ahern, David Ivers, Sandra McAleer, Declan Daly, and to the legendary Frank Crummy and his wife Evelyn. Thanks also to Gerry Curran, the Courts Service and the staff at Dolphin House, Barry Duggan, Ralph Riegel, Jayde Maher, and to Conor O'Donnell, Robert Cox, Aengus O'Hanlon and all my colleagues at the *Irish Mail on Sunday* and DNG Media, .

Finally, thanks to Priscilla, Ainie and Ann Grainger for their time, honestly and openness while reliving at times difficult and traumatic events, which they have managed to overcome with great courage, resilience and dignity.

My deepest gratitude also to other victims of domestic violence whose voices are heard in the narrative but who cannot be identified for legal reasons and their own safety.

PROTECTION AND SAFETY ORDERS

A protection order is an interim order, or a temporary order pending a full hearing for a safety order.

It prevents the use of violence, threats or molestation, watching and besetting. It covers the applicant and their dependent children.

The order can prevent the respondent from communicating to the applicant by electronic means other than access arrangements.

In the event of a suspected breach, gardai have the power to arrest and bring the respondent before a criminal judge.

A safety order is basically a final protection order.

BARRING ORDER

A barring order is a safety order, but where the respondent is barred from the family home.

* Compiled by David Ivers, Legal Executive

* For further information, please contact Stop Domestic Violence in Ireland

ABOUT THE AUTHOR

Shane Doran is a journalist and currently works as News Editor of the *Irish Mail on Sunday.*

He previously edited a newspaper in Cape Town, South Africa and has held senior editorial positions with the *Irish Independent, Sunday Independent, Evening Herald* and *The Irish Daily Star.* He has also worked as a communications consultant and as a publisher of online news platforms.

Shane lives in Inistioge, Co. Kilkenny with his wife and their three dogs.